A Ram
in the Well

To the memory of my two
Welsh grandmothers

A Ram
in the Well

A Welsh Homecoming

JUNE KNOX-MAWER

SUTTON PUBLISHING

This book was first published in 2001 by John Murray
(Publishers) Ltd

This new edition first published in 2004 by
Sutton Publishing Limited · Phoenix Mill
Thrupp · Stroud · Gloucestershire · GL5 2BU

British Library Cataloguing in Publication Data
A catalogue record for this book is available from the British
Library.

ISBN 0 7509 3529 4

Typeset in 11/13pt Photina.
Typesetting and origination by
Sutton Publishing Limited.
Printed and bound in Great Britain by
J.H. Haynes & Co. Ltd, Sparkford.

CONTENTS

AUTHOR'S NOTE

The spirit of this book belongs to all my friends in the valley and beyond, neighbouring families past and present (who may perhaps be better known by other names!). I shall always be grateful for the way they have welcomed me back to Wales, and made our life on the mountain such a rich experience.

Forty years ago I was lucky enough to have my first book accepted by John Murray. Others followed, including some written for other publishers. To be back in the Murray fold with *A Ram in the Well* was for me the happiest of experiences. A book which is so close to my heart could not have been accomplished without the personal encouragement that is the hallmark of this unique publishing house.

Alongside this, a debt of gratitude is owed to my agent, Bruce Hunter of David Higham, another enduring relationship which is rare in the literary world today. As always, I must pay tribute to the skills of my human word-processors, Janet McCormack and Stephen Woosey, for turning my handwritten entanglements into a printed text.

1

BORDERLINES

I still find it hard to believe that my life could be changed forever by an unknown house halfway up a mountain, a house called Hafod.

The name is Welsh for a summer place. Memorably, it was a day of high summer when I discovered it, 30 years ago. Here I was, suddenly realizing that so far I had spent my adult life almost entirely in other people's countries, making my home among strangers in one remote outpost after another, from the deserts of southern Arabia to the islands of the Pacific. Moving between so many wildly different cultures I had to learn to change and adapt. Perhaps I overdid it. Certainly in my youthful enthusiasm I had become the perfect chameleon. As a result, I sometimes felt on my travels that I had mislaid the original self I started out with all those years ago. At last I would be returning to my roots.

Born in Denbighshire, North Wales, it said on my passport. Once abroad though I was classed as British, like everyone else. Both my parents were Welsh even if they sounded as English as possible, as was the custom with professional families in those border parts. As a child, my idea of Wales was that we were in it all right, but only by the skin of our teeth. The view from my bedroom window said it all. Away to the left was a backdrop of dark purple hills, sometimes clear, sometimes veiled, floating behind the rooftops of the town like an oncoming thunder-storm. This was Wales, our Wales anyway. When we drove 'up the mountain' for family expeditions every summer, that mysterious silhouette would all at once be transformed into reality – close-ups of knee-high scratchy heather, stepping-stones in an icy stream, high tea with fresh salmon sandwiches and wimberry tart at the little hotel on top of the moors.

Back at my window, England remained invisible. It was over to the right somewhere, towards the main road that led to Chester and other foreign parts. In bed on winter mornings behind closed curtains, I could hear the miners walking past on their way to Gresford Colliery a few miles along that road, the iron ring of their boots, harsh voices fading, always someone coughing. When I was four, there was a morning when the curtains stayed closed, and were kept closed all day in every front room. Something called a disaster had happened.

'Welsh pit disaster.' At breakfast next day my father read aloud from his newspaper. 'Hundreds feared dead.'

He still hadn't changed out of his dressing-gown into his office suit. Studying his unshaved face, I was shocked to see he was trying not to cry. So this was Wales too, I thought, a place of danger and death. From then onwards, I felt differently about the miners who still passed to work under my window, or trudged back off-shift at the end of the day, eyes and teeth gleaming out of the coal-dust like a tribe of Zulu warriors, and as brave.

It was only when I was much older that I realized how emotionally involved my father was with the North Wales collieries. It was a passion that went back to his youth, long before he set up practice as an accountant. In 1911 his mother had been tragically widowed with seven boys to bring up when her husband, James Ellis, died of TB. Frank was the eldest son. So at sixteen he left school to work as a lowly clerk among the Dickensian ledgers of the main pithead offices at Rhosddu. This must have been humbling, since both his father and his grandfather had held sway there in the all-powerful posts of Agent and Secretary to the company. The real blow was that he lost his chance of going to university and becoming a writer.

Strangely, he seemed to hold no grudge. In the 1930s the traditional Sunday walk of my childhood always took us back to the same now-derelict scene. It was as if the first impact made on his imagination was never to be shaken off. Even his dreams were dominated by the old colliery, or so my mother would tell me.

To me it seemed a world away from our leafy suburban avenue on the other side of town. Sombre and sinister were the slag-heaps on a grey afternoon, the skeletal remains of the winding wheel looming over the broken windows of the Victorian offices. The ritual there was always the same. A stone must be thrown over the parapet of the open shaft and 'counted down' until the echo of a splash came floating up from the bottom of that murky darkness. Then, more cheerfully, my father's hand firm around mine, I would be taken to the nearby field to feed three ancient pit-ponies with lumps of sugar from his pocket.

As we walked, he would be re-telling me the familiar stories. There was the great occasion when he was taken down the pit as a treat on his seventh birthday, squeezed into the creaking cage with the miners. Typically, it was the wretched conditions of the ponies underground that he remembered more clearly than anything else. Another time, out in his father's trap, there was the encounter with a boy of his own age collecting firewood on colliery property. Jokingly, his father told the boy that next time he must either wear his coat longer or cut his sticks shorter.

I never thought of it as a funny story. It made me sad to think of the boy in his handed-down, too-small jacket, probably one of the children from the row of terraced cottages leading out of the colliery gates. From time to time I was taken to visit Number Six by my grandmother's maid, Betty, whose father had been a Rhosddu miner. The tea I was given, with bright orange jelly and Carnation milk, seemed infinitely more festive than the Sunday repast of bread and butter and seed-cake we were always given at my grandmother's house, a 'grace and favour' red-brick villa just round the corner, next to the local chapel.

All this could be regarded as a typically Welsh background. Yet I never thought of it as such, nor was I encouraged to, despite the fact that this particular grandmother was as firmly rooted in North Wales as generations of bourgeois Lloyd-Joneses before her. Her father was a prosperous draper, a local alderman, progressive enough in the 1880s to send his daughter to boarding-school. To me she was simply a tiny old lady with a limp who rattled off stories in an excitable singsong accent that was part of her fascination. Mostly, they were cautionary tales of childhood disobedience and disaster featuring a whole tribe of uncles, great-uncles, and cousins-once-removed.

'These Ellises! These Lloyd-Joneses!'

My mother's sigh was one of exasperation as she took down, yet again, the sepia family photographs my father liked to hang on the landing. She prided herself on her English maiden name of Renfrey which was, in fact, inescapably Celtic. Her father had come from Cornwall as a young man to settle in Pembrokeshire. (Again I hear my mother's voice – 'Little England Beyond Wales'.) But he married a girl who was pure rural South Wales, a gamekeeper's daughter from Carmarthenshire. Grannie Renfrey was another born story-teller, though I never heard her speak Welsh. Perhaps she put it behind her when she married. But the family network was still strong. Of all the summer holidays at her house by the sea, I remember best the visits to farm kitchens with salted bacon hanging from the beams, a hymn-book open on the parlour piano, and outside in the fields a strong seductive smell I was told was manure.

Under the surface of this Anglo-Welsh world of mine there lurked a hidden fault-line. I only became aware of it when I started at the local Grammar School for Girls. It was a famous institution with an imposing headmistress who wore a hat trimmed with cherries and who had once been painted by Augustus John. Welsh was taught as a special subject but only to those who already spoke the language. Their studies were conducted at a lofty, academic level, or so it seemed to the rest of us, the *déclassée* non-speakers, Welsh-born but deemed sadly lacking in national pride.

Fortunately, we had a teacher of English Literature, the maverick Miss Wynne-Jones, who did something to redress the balance. Winnie had a passion for the Anglo-Welsh poets. She claimed they had captured the essence of the Welsh Spirit far better than their Cymric counterparts.

'Mongrel blood, you see,' she told us. 'Such vitality.'

We felt uplifted, especially when she quoted from her special favourite, Gerard Manley Hopkins, her voice swooning with emotion.

Lovely the woods, waters, meadows, combes, vales,
All the air things wear that build this world of Wales . . .

After a pause, her tone would sharpen for the next line, spectacles glinting in what seemed to be my direction . . .

'only the inmate does not correspond . . .'

Officially there was a choice on the syllabus between Welsh and French.

'French will be much more useful to you,' I was told when I daringly suggested joining the Welsh speakers who always had that enviable air of a chosen race about them.

Some of them were my friends but their ability to swing

carelessly from one language to another somehow set them apart. I knew that the English poems I submitted for the school Eisteddfods would never make the grade for the Bardic Chair. The stars of St David's Day were always the harp-players and the penillion-singers, warbling through the complexities of counter-melodies, smiling coyly for the photographers in their witches' hats and red shawls and idiotic frilly aprons. These were the girls who came in by early morning bus from the hill farms and the mining villages, Morfydd from Minera, Ceridwen from Caergwrle, Bethan from Bwlchgwyn, girls with muddy black stockings and satchels stuffed with extra homework and lunch-time sandwiches in greaseproof paper. In the cloakrooms they gabbled together like flocks of starlings. But once at their desks they became model pupils, hunched over their books in furious concentration, scribbling down their Cicero translations as if their lives depended on it. No doubt they did. Whatever their backgrounds, the cleverest of them already had their sights set on Bangor and Aberystwyth, true daughters of the old Welsh passion for education and improvement.

At seventeen, I actually got as far as Aberystwyth myself for what was known as a scholarship interview. But once again I was turned in a 'more useful' direction. If I wanted to be a writer, I should start as a cub reporter with a local newspaper, preferably an English one. The editor of the *Chester Chronicle*, a distinguished figure in his eighties, was kind enough to take me on.

Every day the journey to work took me across that camouflaged green border into another country. Every day I was aware of leaving Wales a little bit further behind. Within the first few miles, though, the bus went past a Gresford colliery that was nationalized and flourishing again. At that moment it was hard not to flinch a little at the thought of the miners whose bodies still lay entombed far below the surface of that noisy main road.

But soon I was too busy thinking about my job. As a

budding social reporter, I worked overtime for my £4 pay-packet, laboriously polishing up my accounts of hunt balls, flower shows in the cathedral close, the New Look fashions worn by the ladies in the Duke of Westminster's box at Chester races.

Our editorial offices did not exactly accord with the image of a dignified county newspaper. Tucked away in a warren of rickety buildings at the back of the Rows, we juniors wrote our pieces around a shabby Victorian dining-table, with two type-writers and one telephone between us. Every now and then Mr Parker, our venerable editor, came creaking down from his attic room followed by his Thurberesque Airedale dog, Dinah. When they had checked on our progress, there might be an invitation to tea at Bollands Restaurant, for the young ladies at least. Here a palm court trio played Ivor Novello and Mr P recounted the story of his famous coup. As a youthful reporter, he had apparently scooped the world press with the news of Gladstone's death.

'It was only because I knew a short cut to Hawarden post office,' he explained modestly.'Short cuts, that's the thing, Miss Ellis.' From under his eyebrows, he would glance sharply at my dog-eared reporter's notebook. 'Not too many adverbs and adjectives. It's a Welsh failing, of course,' he liked to add, by way of consolation.

Usually the office-boy ran to and fro with our copy between the sub-editors and the printing works at the end of the alley-way. Sometimes, if there was a last-minute correction, I took it along myself. It was always an awesome experience to climb the iron stairs to The Works. Inside, the clatter of arcane machinery and the heady whiff of hot metal were thrilling reminders that I was a small part of this secret powerhouse of activity. The printers themselves, perched at their Linotype keyboards, were inky, lugubrious figures not given to idle chat. But they always bent an ear to my hoarse pleas to 'squeeze in the last line if you possibly can'.

Miraculously, when the Friday editions thundered out

from the press, there it would be, tucked in at the bottom of the page. One week I saw that, for the first time, I had a column to myself with my name on it. With the paper warm in my hand, I felt my heart thumping in time with the giant rollers. I knew it was one of those moments not to be forgotten, whatever else the future might hold.

As a teenager, I was still living at home with my parents . . . Three years later Wales had somehow moved from the other side of the border to the other side of the world. Or rather, I had moved. It was a dramatic transformation. The hopeful journalist had turned into a barrister's wife. Then, even stranger, she found she was a colonial memsahib married to a judge. At least there was a reassuring sense of continuity about the fact that Ronnie was from my home town, someone I'd known since schooldays, and his family too. Ahead of him lay a life of alarming and sometimes bizarre responsibilities, especially for one so young. For me the sense of unreality continued, as if I had been plunged into some long-running fancy-dress party. Memories of Wales faded like old-fashioned snapshots alongside the Technicolor slides of travels in Arabia, tea-parties with the sultan's harem, desert picnics by moonlight, the end-of-Empire soirées and parades.

Moving to live in Fiji in the Sixties added new elements of fantasy. Was the King of Tonga's coronation under the palm-trees only a dream? Did they exist in reality, the dancers in their bird-of-paradise plumage, the *kava* ceremonies with their hypnotic drumming and chanting, those landfalls at dawn on the long sea journeys from one atoll to another?

Fortunately, over the decades, there were all the intervening periods of real life to keep my feet on the ground. Our two children were born. I wrote travel books. I learned to broadcast. There were the usual doldrums of rainy seasons, heat exhaustion, bouts of social boredom, family separations and homesickness.

When it was time to leave I felt a different kind of homesickness begin. There was the sadness of separation from happy shores and familiar faces, especially those which had become part of the domestic scene. The trunks and the packing cases were taken aboard for the last time. The figures on the wharf were waving, then diminishing, as the ship drew away for the long journey home.

But, back in this country again, where was home? Childhood memories were not enough to sustain a new life. Our own children were teenagers now, one at boarding school, the other about to leave, with luck, for university. Our parents still lived in the same border town and, as ever, would give us a base while we debated the future. Professionally, Liverpool then London would be the focal points for both our careers. But in all these shifting prospects, there had to be one fixed compass-point. In my heart I knew it could only be Wales.

2

A House Called Summer

'A place in Wales?' Friends sounded dubious when the idea was mentioned. 'You mean a weekend cottage?'

It wasn't at all what I meant. That expression meant 'leisure breaks', a drop-out point for people who simply wanted to get away from somewhere else. Their Wales was a place to sail and climb mountains and enjoy a Sunday barbecue before loading up the car again for the bumper-to-bumper drive back over the border to the rat-race of urban life.

'But isn't that just what you'll be doing,' someone pointed out, 'relaxing for a few days, then off again back to reality in London or wherever?'

It may well have looked like that. The difference was that I wanted my reality to be rooted in Wales. Work would obviously dictate limits to the time we could spend there. But it might not always be so. I had a dream of a house to call home, somewhere with an endless future, a place to work at and plan around, a place to love, I suppose. Above all, what I wanted was a foothold in my own country and the chance to be an insider at last.

It was an appealing picture. *The Exile's Return*, the artist would have titled it a hundred years ago. It was the kind of theme dear to the Victorian heart and I could see it clearly down to the last Pre-Raphaelite detail – the ivy tendrils round the cottage door, the wistful wanderer at the gate (with faithful dog), over the hills a rainbow. The missing piece of the dream was the house itself. Did such a haven exist? There were practical considerations. It had to be within reach of a train to take R to court and me to the BBC, yet it had to be off the beaten track, unspoiled Welsh in style and setting. Also, it had to be cheap because a working flat in London must also be paid for.

Obviously the first place to start looking was in the property columns of the North Wales papers. But I found it hard to concentrate on the effusive advertisements of the local estate agent and the glossy brochures that came showering through the letterboxes of our parental homes in Wrexham. None of them matched the idea in my head. Besides, I had the feeling I would be given a sign of some kind if I would only leave things to fate. Just as the legendary Library Angel guides the reader towards the most elusive book, there must also be a Property Angel hovering over the unknown house that is the perfect answer to our prayers. You just had to keep your psychic antennae turned in the right direction.

That afternoon in July we were drawn back to old haunts, driving around the Denbighshire moors of my childhood. There was no sign of angelic wings, only a buzzard floating high overhead with that melancholy mewing call of his. Was he following us or were we following him as he circled down over the valley that lay in the shadow of the old mountain pass? The road ahead led on into the famous Vale of Llangollen, whose beauty had thrown the nineteenth-century literary visitors into such ecstasies, Hazlitt, Coleridge, Wordsworth and Ruskin and, of course, the peripatetic George Borrow. Then suddenly, to the left, a village sign-post caught my eye. Beneath it, half-buried in a hedge was a notice-board with the words, 'Cottage For Sale Half a Mile Ahead'. There was an arrow pointing downhill in the opposite direction. A winding track disappeared into the shade of overhanging trees. We got out to take a closer look. There was no sign of a cottage or any other abode. Then a faint breeze rustled the stillness. Through the branches there was a glimpse of something white in the distance, halfway up the opposite mountain. From where we stood, it looked not so much like a house as a small ship lying stranded in a sea of bracken.

We looked at each other. It seemed a momentous sighting. 'Silent, upon a peak in Darien' were the words that sprang to mind.

'What do you think?'

'Might as well take a look.'

'Why not?'

Because the prospect appeared too good to be true we said no more and got back into the car. In the silence the engine seemed to take a deep breath. The next minute we were plunging forward down the lane in a jolting helter-skelter rush, six-foot-deep in purple foxgloves and white cow-parsley. A furious barking broke out as we passed a sleepy-looking farmhouse, though no one seemed to be about. At the bottom of the hill the track became a bridge with a brook swirling away on either side and a tumbledown witch's cottage, crouched under some elderberry trees.

On up the next switchback there was another farm. This time the dogs came running out to us, a black and white tangle of them, snapping at the heels of the four-wheeled animal which refused to be cornered. A U-turn came next, and then a lop-sided gate tied up with red binder-twine. The *Marie Celeste* on the mountainside had mysteriously disappeared from view, but there was another arrow on the back of the gate, this time saying simply 'Hafod'. It was like following the clues in a treasure hunt. It was time to get out and walk, it seemed. The path ahead was full of ruts, and steep too, though I think it was excitement that made me breathless.

As we walked, the scene that opened up in front of us was far too remarkable to be called a view. We were at the heart of a succession of high wooded slopes that folded away in the haze as far as the eye could see. A narrow valley lay cupped between them and just below us a river went winding through towards a scattering of distant rooftops. Hedges, lanes and fields all hung at a slant. The beauty of it was dream-like.

But all the time I was looking for Hafod. I remembered the name was traditionally used for a place on high ground where sheep are sent to graze in the summer. As if on cue, a flock of them materialized on the bank below, a line of disapproving faces poking out of the bracken to inspect us. But there was still no sign of the house.

Then suddenly there it was, hiding away at our backs on the other side of the track. Now, through the trees, I could see three chimneys, a whitewashed front, small windows that squinted out at the amazing view as if it was nothing to be impressed about. The long slate roof looked more accustomed to rain than sun. The general impression was distinctly plain, rather than picturesque. It was only when closer, climbing up the path at the side, I realized that the extraordinary thing about the house was the way it had been built. Somehow or other it had been wedged tight into the steep angle of the land so that it looked like part of the mountain itself, as firmly rooted as the oaks and the rocks and the yellow gorse around it.

A wicket-gate had the letters, Hafod, nailed crookedly across the top. I put my hand on it and waited a moment to introduce myself. There was such a strong sense of disturbing a sleep of some kind, as if something or someone had decided to withdraw here forever and let the rest of the world go by.

On a gentle push, the gate creaked open. I led the way up the overgrown path to a rough stone terrace patched with moss and dandelions. This was where the house began. Propped against the front wall stood an iron bench that must surely have been the property of the Great Western Railway fifty years before. We both collapsed on it to draw breath. Sitting there in the sunshine, we felt like passengers on some abandoned country platform. All around us the station-master's roses were running riot and the view of the green valley fields was as unreal as a pre-war touring poster. Behind us, Hafod itself had the air of an ancient train that had come to rest in some forgotten siding in the forest.

We couldn't get into it, of course. Inside a front porch made of shaky trellis-work the door was firmly locked. But peering through the dust of the window panes I could see that it was a train without a corridor, one room apparently leading straight into another. There seemed to be four or five of them, first-class at the centre where flowery paper denoted parlour and dining-room, third-class at each end for hall, kitchen and bathroom. Upstairs remained a mystery. We could just see that there were two tiny staircases leading up from each end of the house to what might be three or even four bedrooms, judging by the upper windows, small as they were.

There would be more clues at the back of the house though. Warily we followed separate tracks. The way I went, it was only just possible to squeeze my way round. Because here was another Hafod eccentricity. The back of the place was encircled by a massive dry-stone wall, almost as high as the roof, no doubt built to protect the inhabitants against landslides. In fact it seemed to be shoring up the whole mountain, so that edging along the narrow gap between wall and house produced an eerie hint of claustrophobia. Overhanging ferns and ivy clung thickly between the stones, making a tunnel of greenish light. Here was an earthy secretive smell that seemed to belong to a different Hafod. Moss had grown underfoot and the various doors were apparently disused. The last of them, however, opened onto an old privy which I was startled to find engaged. Inside was a rumpled-looking tawny owl. Both of us froze, staring at one another in some embarrassment. The silence was broken by an irritable old man's cough. Then, turning his head, the sitting tenant spread his wings and floated off into the trees.

I had come to some steps that led up to the bank behind the house. From here, you could almost walk across onto the roof. The sun had turned the slates to silver and the weatherworn surface sloped and rippled like a beach when the tide is out. All around us were tangled thickets of blackberry brambles and wild roses, overgrown gooseberry bushes and rampant raspberries, dog-daisies and willow-herb, a sleeping-beauty wilderness of thorn and flower that it was almost impossible to penetrate. Here and there you could see the remains of netting and fencing, the odd iron post marking a lost pathway. The ghosts of other people's gardens, I thought, generations of them. Despite the sunshine, there was a melancholy about them, an air of decline and fall after the expenditure of so much endeavour.

But here we were, intent on new beginnings. In that brilliant mountain air, optimism surged. Settled in such a place, anything was possible. Hafod could take over our lives, hazards and all.

'The freedom of it! Talk about paradise!'

'The track up would have to be repaired . . .'

'A sort of secret valley! The last of *Wild Wales!*'

'You could be completely cut off, of course. Think of the bad weather.'

'Think of the good! And look – '

In the copse at the top of the bank, I had spotted a cascade of scarlet berries.

'A rowan tree,' I said, as if that clinched everything. I had read that, in the old days, one was planted in most gardens to protect the house and its inhabitants against witchcraft and the various spiteful fairies of Welsh folklore.

'A mountain ash, isn't it?'

'Same thing.'

But now we were in a hurry to get away. We needed to make a note of the agent's name on the For Sale notice that had caught my eye in the first place. Strangely enough we could see no such sign on display at the house, but perhaps that was to avoid the risk of anyone's breaking in. Perhaps they could tell us more at one of the farms we had passed.

Outside the farmyard, the dogs were quiet this time, crouched at the feet of their owner. A thin grey-haired man he was, a reassuring figure in his old canvas jacket ready for milking. He had a quizzical smile for us as he watched the car stop at the gate.

'Been to open up the place then, have you?'

Alas, we had no keys, I told him. But we'd had a good look round outside. A fascinating place, we thought. Wonderful view.

He nodded, still smiling. 'Not that you can live on a view, though. None of us can do that. Davis is the name,' he went on. 'Pen-y-bryn.'

As we shook hands, his wife came out to join us, a neat figure in pinny and wellingtons, milk-bucket in hand.

'Well, we hope you'll be very happy up there, anyway,' she put in tactfully.

'I'm sure we shall if we get the place,' R said.

'*If* you get the place –'

The smiles faded, anxious looks were exchanged, followed by a flurry of Welsh. I felt a qualm of foreboding.

'Sorry,' Mr Davis said eventually. 'We thought you were the new owners. With the sale this morning, isn't it?'

For once, the Welsh habit of turning a statement into a question lacked charm. The possibility of doubt only added to the awful suspense. Besides, Mrs Davis had rushed into the house and was now emerging with a newspaper in her hand.

'And you didn't know.' Her face quivered with sympathy as she thrust the cutting into my hand. 'There you are, see.'

Only too clearly we saw the notice of a property sale by auction to take place in a Chester hotel at 11 a.m. this very day. Hafod was 'a converted Welsh cottage of unique appeal, commanding unrivalled views across the surrounding hills and valleys . . . '

By now it would be the prized possession of some wretched interlopers from over the border, I thought unfairly. There would be a Georgian-style conservatory and cocktail parties on the terrace within months.

Mr Davis must have read my feelings.

'They do like our Welsh scenery,' he said, 'and who can blame them? Besides, the last people who lived there were from England too, fair play.' That phrase *chwarae teg* was a useful one, I noted to myself, especially in the circumstances.

'And you too?' prompted Mrs Davis gently.

'I'm Welsh.' The waves of disappointment made it hard not to sound emotional. 'And my husband,' I added. 'Half anyway.'

'Well then!' The phrase hung in the air, warm with approval. 'Another time, I'm sure.'

'We'll keep a look-out for you,' called Mr Davis as we drove away. 'These places do come up from time to time . . . '

But not a place like Hafod, I thought. As the car turned onto the road from the Pass again, it was possible to catch a last glimpse of the house, reduced to a white dot in the folds of the mountain. But I didn't want to look. It was too painful. It had been not so much love at first sight as sheer infatuation, the kind of thing that makes excuses for any faults and shortcomings, however serious.

'Anyway,' I said, 'we may have lost a house but we've found friends.'

'And perhaps we should be more systematic about the whole thing,' came the voice next to me. 'Forget impulse buying. Make some lists, make contacts.'

I agreed. 'Starting tomorrow.'

Tomorrow started with the crumpled cutting in my pocket. The Chester estate agents would be as good a first contact as any other, better perhaps. Secretly, I suppose, I was interested in the sale price of Hafod, hoping it would be well beyond anything we could have afforded.

The voice at the end of the phone was as blasé as it was non-committal. Yes, there was a house in Denbighshire up for auction yesterday.

'We get so many of these old Welsh cottages. Most of them in dire need of modernization and refurbishment.' He laughed. 'Despite what the owners tell you.' There was a pause. 'I'll just have to check the records.'

There was another pause.

When the voice came back, I had to ask him to repeat the message. I still couldn't believe my ears. The reserve price had not been reached. The property had been withdrawn.

'It's still on the market, then?'

The man from the agency must have picked up the note of eager disbelief in my voice. His own perked up considerably as he went on to explain that it was a fairly modest figure anyway. The house was simply too remote to attract the right kind of buyer. Perhaps I was that very buyer, he suggested, in which case I must make haste with my offer because the owner, a lady of advanced years, was considering an alternative plan to let the house to holiday tenants. Such tenants were already lined up and interested. But an appointment could be made for me to call into the Chester office to discuss terms for the purchase of Hafod . . .

Hafod. The magic name was written in smudged copper-plate on the label of the large iron key that was handed over to me the very next day in exchange for £12,000. I kept opening my bag in joyous disbelief to inspect it, as I sat in the train going back to Wrexham. I had never made out a cheque of that size in my whole life. The estate agent's precious receipt was further proof of the miracle. So was the sale brochure I had been given.

Poring over it as we jolted over the border into Wales again, I was discovering the clues to various mysteries . . .

water supply from a well on the hill, the origins of the train-shape design which went back to the days when it was a row of three up-and-downs. But for whom had they been built? Who were the three Misses Sinclair who had last occupied them?

The views were much dwelt on. 'Views are panoramic, though access is difficult.'

There were also some impressive descriptions of the interior, mention of vestibules, exposed rafters, recessed china-cabinets and the like. In smaller print came the warning that some refurbishment would be needed to bring the domestic arrangements up to required standards. It was a disturbing reminder that we had not actually been inside the house. Then I remembered the Property Angel. Having guided us so far, I felt sure I could rely on his good offices to see us through. And there was always the rowan tree, in case of real trouble . . .

3

VACANT POSSESSION

Taking possession of a property is a phrase with a solemn ring to it. To me it meant the act of crossing my Welsh threshold for the first time, a stirring moment I had rehearsed in my imagination more than once. I should have guessed that Hafod rarely conforms to expectations.

This time I was on my own and it was raining. A car from Wrexham brought me up, with a lugubrious driver who said he wouldn't live out in the sticks if you paid him. As he rattled away down the track, I had to agree that the valley was not looking its best. The rain was no ordinary downpour either, but a Welsh speciality known as *niwl*, a spectral drizzle that floats along horizontally like ectoplasm. Over the mountain slopes dense cloud billowed down to meet it. As a result I found myself in the gloaming at midday, an eerie experience after the golden weather of our first visit. Strangest of all was the way the dazzling views had been extinguished as if they never were. It was rather like visiting a famous stately home to find every room shrouded in dust-covers while the place was being refurbished.

Even more disconcerting was the discovery that I seemed unable to take possession of Hafod after all. Surrounded by bags and baggage, I stood beneath the dripping porch feeling distinctly rebuffed. The old iron key from the agents simply refused to let me in. After a couple of fruitless efforts I realized it bore no relation at all to the lock on the door, which was comparatively new. It seemed I had been given the wrong key. So where was the right one? Somewhere inside, no doubt, with the complete set of house keys which had been deposited 'for safety' in the old bread oven, or so I had been told.

There was no point in further wrestling and breaking in was out of the question. Only a gymnastic squirrel could squeeze in through those criss-cross window-panes. My spirits sank. To a superstitious soul like mine, it was a bad omen. The message was that I was not welcome. Entry to paradise was barred.

Then common sense intervened. There must be another door, the back door obviously. I tried to remember seeing such a thing on last week's visit, but failed. I had been too carried away to take note of such practical details.

This time, holding my breath, I began to edge my way round the back wall from the opposite direction. Suddenly there it was, half-hidden by brambles, just the right kind of door, very heavy, very old. Beneath layers of peeling black paint there seemed to be a variety of disused bolts and latches, also an ancient door-knocker in the shape of a sphinx's head. One of the spinster ladies must have been a traveller in antique lands. This was my good omen, I decided. With a quick prayer to the gods I thrust the key into the most likely-looking aperture.

It turned quite easily. I pushed hard and there was a grating sound as the bottom of the door scraped over the uneven floor. Years ago it must have dropped on its hinges and then been left to lean there, resting. But at least I was over the threshold, suddenly nervous, but impatient to find what awaited me.

Inside, the place was bare of everything except the past. The slate flagstones spoke of that. So did the crumbling plaster in the passageway and the crooked rafters overhead. You could sniff it in the air too – the ashes of innumerable smoky fires, pipe-tobacco that took me back to my South Wales grandfather, salted bacon, wet sheepdogs, and sour working clothes, hung from the pegs to dry. Somehow the lady-like Misses Sinclair had disappeared. In their wake all the old people had taken over again, the generations of labouring families who had made their home here for the past two hundred years.

A rusty tap dripped into the stone sink in the corner. The range had been dismembered but the original bread oven next to it revealed the promised bunch of keys. Walking on through the other rooms, I found a new element in possession – the damp. It seemed to have settled not just in the air but deep in the skin and bones of the house. Flowered wallpaper hung down in melancholy strips, ashamed at the glimpses of blue distemper underneath. Further on there were latter-day 'improvements' like the linoleum that curled away from the walls, leaving the odd puddle behind. The smell now was of mould, dry rot too. This was damp on a Gothic scale.

In my imagination it was seeping in from the earth of the mountain at the back of us, right down to the roots of the trees in the little copse that had clambered and twined their way down to the house like one of those woodcut illustrations to a Grimm's fairy-tale.

The reality was far from poetical. I reminded myself that this was the house I planned to settle into this very day. Such was my enthusiasm that Mr Rhys and his removal van had been booked to deliver our worldly goods to Hafod within the next hour. Summoning courage, I climbed the two staircases, one at each end of the house, counted the four bedrooms, checked to see if the roof was leaking anywhere. But no, the damp was of natural not man-made origin. Beneath the beams the spiders' webs and their inhabitants looked fairly dry. There was the same mildewed chill in the air, though, with daylight reduced to a mottled sepia. It occurred to me that even when our radiators arrived, there would be no electricity to warm the place. The power had been switched off on the departure of the last inhabitants. Then I reminded myself that I had counted no less than three fireplaces downstairs. Matches, and even candles and a paraffin lamp were tucked away at the bottom of one of my bags of basic supplies (including whisky), something I'd learned from our travels in the rain-swept highlands of Fiji. Might there not be wood, perhaps even some coal, left behind in one of the many Hafod outhouses?

Out in the soggy garden, I climbed up a path or two. The first door I opened let loose an avalanche of the kind of junk that would thrill the heart of any future archaeologist. Who were the Welsh would be the familiar question, those long-vanished mountain-dwellers of the north called the *Gogledd*? What mysterious instinct led them to treasure these ancestral hoards of broken artefacts, the buckets with holes, the rakes without handles, the saw with no teeth, the much-stained china pot adorned with pink roses? Why were the empty paint-tins still preserved in battered heaps, the rusty lamps kept hanging on their nails next to a strange mud-caked garment mummified by age into the shape of its original owner? Peering in from the rain, I thought I knew the answers. In remote parts like this, it would be hard to throw anything away, 'just in case' and no doubt the Welsh cling more obstinately than most to these reminders of other times. Besides, out here in the wilds, how would you actually dispose of such things?

Weeks later I was to discover that burial was the usual solution as some interesting finds came to light on the mountainside. Meanwhile I was searching for fuel for my fire. Another shed, a few steps further up, looked promising. An old treadle sewing-machine blocked the doorway. Behind it lurked the remains of a piano, its yellowing ivories bared in a sepulchral grin. But there in the corner, half-smothered in ivy, was a small stack of logs together with what looked like the witches' cauldron from *Macbeth*. Miraculously, there was still some coal in the bottom.

It was all I needed. The wood was dry. Together with a few scraps of newspaper lining a kitchen drawer – (a wartime *Radio Times*, as it happened, an archive in itself) I soon had the beginnings of a fire. It was the room I wistfully envisaged as the parlour. Once the chill had gone, I could put the sofa in the front of the blaze, with some rugs for sleeping that night, provided that J Rhys and Sons successfully made their way up the abyss.

Would I be nervous in the house alone, I wondered? Strangely enough there was already no real sense of being 'on my own' at Hafod. As I sat back on my heels, treasuring my first fire, I even had a sense of company, of a shadowy kind. So many lives had been lived in these little rooms, three separate households packed into the row of tiny cottages, it was not hard to imagine a footstep on the stair, the sound of a door opening, voices on the other side of the wall. Here was yet another newcomer, they seemed to say, come to make her own changes, no doubt. It might be worth keeping an eye on her anyway, see how she gets on in the old place.

So it was not an unwelcoming atmosphere. Kindly almost, I would have said. Nevertheless, it was reassuring to remind myself that I did have flesh-and-blood neighbours in the shape of Mr and Mrs Davis. There was no one around at Pen-y-Bryn when the car went past. But I decided there was no need to leave a note on the door to say I had arrived. Besides, the dogs were already defending the gate at the sight of strangers. They'd probably heard the news like the rest of the valley. The Welsh bush-telegraph would have been passing the word around ever since I'd written my name on the cheque. Even now, as I unpacked my bags for my iron rations, there was a knock on the door, a friendly-sounding triple tattoo.

In the porch stood Will Davis, his cheerful face poking out of soaked oilskins.

'Seen smoke from the chimney. You got the place then – fair play!'

A wet handshake was thrust forward. But no, he

wouldn't come in. 'I'm after an old ram got caught in a fence higher up. But just to say that Rhys the Remove's on his way.' The words came faster and more furious. 'Only this minute had a call from Wyn Williams on the other side of the Pass. He'd got the word from Tom Lewis further back. One of those great big what-d'you-call pantecknik things went past a minute ago.' He glanced down at the track, shaking his head. 'Whether he'll make it though – '

I tried not to sound as alarmed as I felt. 'But I told him specially. Nothing big, just a couple of pickup trucks.'

Mr Davis clicked his tongue in sympathy. 'That's old Rhys for you. Always knows best. Still, trust in God, isn't it?'

'Will you be calling on your way back?' I asked hopefully.

Again Mr Davis shook his head. 'Got the Land Rover meeting me down by the brook.' He saluted me with the long crook he was carrying, then held out a small can of milk. 'Nearly forgot. Megan said you'd be needing some. Tomorrow though, you'll come down for a *paned* she says.'

'A what?'

'Cup of tea, bit of a chat.' He gave his courteous smile. 'You'll be all right, then?'

'Of course,' I told him. Then he was off, ducking away into the rain again. Watching him go, I could see one or two cars on the Pass with their lights on, in the gloom of the afternoon. They seemed to be making way for the kind of towering vehicle that could only be Mr Rhys's pantechnicon. Horns were hooting and across the valley could be heard the swelling vibration of a mighty engine.

Inside my head, a similar throbbing had begun. Seriously unnerved, I retreated to the kitchen to swallow two aspirin with some tea from my thermos. Even there I could hear the dogs in full cry. Men's voices joined in, a crescendo of Welsh oaths mingled with the mournful lowing of distracted heifers. Negotiating the lane between the two farms, the pantechnicon had obviously created havoc with their stately afternoon procession to the milking sheds.

I held my breath. The worst was yet to come – the notorious U-turn and then the edge-of-the-mountain track up to Hafod. This time conscience drove me to the door. Mercifully the van was out of sight at this stage, hidden by trees. The panting and groaning of the engine grew louder. Progress seemed indicated just for a second or so, before there came the wrenching sound of lift-off followed by impact, then a shuddering descent into silence. I opened my eyes again. I now had an unbroken view of the slowly-tilting colossus where it had come to rest against the wall of the barn below the house. 'Here Comes Rhys' announced the brightly-painted slogan across the front.

I hurried back into the kitchen. After all, what could I do to help? Within minutes I would hear Mr Rhys's own report on the situation.

Sure enough, even as I added a quick dash of whisky to the remains of my tea, there was the man himself at the kitchen window. Surprisingly, he looked flushed with success.

'Got her up here, anyway!' was his cheerful cry as I went out to meet him. 'Bit of a problem with the old barn,' he went on. 'But from what I hear it's due to come down anyway so what's a few stones here and there.'

I tried to remonstrate but his grin only grew broader. No trouble at all with the lurry (the local word for all heavy transport) he claimed. They'd soon have her back on her feet once the stuff inside had been taken out. Under his beetling black brows, Mr Rhys's eyes sparkled with the drama of it all.

'Got my boys with me. Carry everything up, they will, in no time at all.'

Two striplings in tee-shirts were already staggering in under some kitchen boxes and a stack of chairs. The rain had now changed direction and was wafting in through the open door.

'Should be all right for water up here, anyway,' said Mr Rhys.

Spring water, I boasted. Fresh from the well up the mountain. I turned on the tap to demonstrate. With much clanking and grinding a brown stream gushed out then stopped.

Mr Rhys was reassuring. 'These old pipes. Get a bit rusty over the years.' He blew vigorously into the tap for a few minutes. A belch or two followed from Mr R and the tap. Slowly some clearer water trickled through, enough for me to fill the kettle and make tea for us all on the primus stove while my guest ran through his family history (wagoners and wheelrights) and the budding talents of his sons (brilliant musicians, natural comedians). Halfway through there came the cry of an abandoned lamb, several abandoned lambs, gathered near the back door.

'Left the gate open did you, Gareth?' he demanded accusingly. 'Or was it you, Gwyn, more likely?'

The two of them fled. I followed to see a gaggle of ewes munching their way through some downtrodden lobelia, no doubt part of the 'Well Established Alpine Rock Garden' left behind by the Misses Sinclair. By the time they had been seen off with their offspring, it was time for the real removal business to begin. The rain had stopped and it was decreed that a start would be made with the beds. Luckily they were all singles.

'Have to go through the windows, though,' Mr Rhys announced. He had already inspected the staircases. 'Hell of a job getting a coffin up them, let alone a bed.'

Ropes were found and he disappeared upstairs to orchestrate the operation. I beat another cowardly retreat to the kitchen to make more tea. When Mr R reappeared he was breathing heavily, a puzzled look on his face.

'Something missing here.'

My heart sank.

'Stairs,' he went on, mopping his neck. 'Should be three lots of them, surely, not two.'

The same thought had occurred to me. Although at some stage the three up-and-downs had been knocked through on the ground floor to make a single house, the stairs to the two end cottages had been left intact. There was a middle bedroom all right, but no sign of the original way up to it. In the parlour we stared up at a small cross-beam in the corner of the ceiling. Mr Rhys declared it to be, without doubt, the site of the old stairwell.

'Or they might just have managed with a ladder to climb up to bed. Lots of people did in those days, farm labourers, quarrymen's families, with all their kids to fit in.'

He paused to watch his own offspring lurching to and fro with our hand-me-down tables and chests, also a grandfather clock with no pendulum.

'Anyway.' He gave me a wink. 'It's what the property people would call a character feature all right. One house downstairs but upstairs you've got two. Will you keep it like that or open it up?'

Keep it as it is, I decided. It would be just another Hafod idiosyncrasy. And more useful with family and visitors anyway, I told him.

He rolled his eyes. 'Besides, if you went through you might find a body. One of them walled-up nuns, like in haunted houses.'

Right now the bathroom was the place for bodies, it seemed. No less than four deceased mice have been discovered in a cupboard containing a much-gnawed hot-water bottle and an empty packet of indigestion powder.

'Must have been desperate,' said Gareth.

'More like a mass suicide,' said Gwyn, bringing out the remains of a tin of mouse poison.

They fell about laughing. But Mr Rhys brought them back to order.

'Right then! Just a few more pieces at the back and we're finished.'

Last in was the cabin trunk, a period piece with its leather straps and peeling patchwork of P & O labels.

'Open it up for you, shall we?' called Mr Rhys. I caught an

edge of curiosity in his voice. 'Save you trouble with these old locks. Is there a key?'

'No key,' I called back from upstairs. 'You may need a screwdriver though.'

For the next minute or so there was the sound of hammering followed by the creak of rusty hinges and the rustle of packing straw. Then silence fell.

'Funny old stuff they've got here,' said a low voice.

More rustling gave way to stifled mirth. I looked down over the stair-rail to see Mr Rhys brandishing a Fijian war-club. Gareth and Gwyn had found a pair of grass skirts and were improvising a *hula*. The performance froze into a guilty tableau.

'Sorry,' chuckled Mr Rhys. 'Fancy dress, is it?'

It seemed a pity to spoil the party with a travel lecture. Souvenirs, actually, I explained, the kind of things you brought back with you to remind you of the past. We'd been living in the South Sea islands for almost twelve years – Fiji, Tonga, the Gilbert and Ellice, Nauru . . .

I trailed off. Mr Rhys was pondering the correct response to this unlikely information.

'Did you like the district?' he inquired. And then, 'Bit cut off, I suppose.'

I agreed that it could be, but no more than Hafod perhaps.

I was busy unearthing the rest of our trophies. Laid out in the grey light of a rain-swept house in Wales, they looked strangely faded and forlorn, those dancing-fans with their scarlet feathers, the hangings of painted barkcloth, the ceremonial necklaces of shark's teeth and mother-of-pearl. Finally, the great wooden *kava* bowl from Bau was unwrapped. Mr Rhys took a closer look at the curious pronged objects tucked inside, holding them up to the light.

'Cannibal forks,' I explained.

Mr Rhys kept his nerve. 'Funny shape, aren't they?'

You were not supposed to touch human flesh with your

fingers while you were eating it, I told him. '"Long-pig" they used to call it when it was cooked.'

Gareth swallowed. 'Did you ever meet one? A cannibal, I mean.'

I thought of the old man in that smoky little hut up in the hills of Vanua Levu. He had giggled, half-ashamed, as he told me how as a boy he had been made to eat a piece of an enemy body in those days of tribal warfare. 'Before the Mission.'

'Yes, there was one,' I replied. 'He said the best part was the elbow.'

'Wouldn't get much off yours, Dad,' quipped Gwyn. Gareth was fingering his Welsh dragon tattoo. This time the mirth was just a little uneasy, I thought. The forks were replaced in the bowl and Mr Rhys had the last line as he made for the kitchen. 'You'll want these in here then.'

In the doorway Gareth looked at his watch. They had a gig tonight he reminded his brother and they had to pick up their guitars. I asked if it was folk music they played.

Gwyn shrugged, tucked a trailing lock behind one ear. 'Depends. If it's Wrexham, it's the Sex Pistols. If it's Bala we do the protest stuff, "Owain Glyndŵr Rules OK" kind of thing.'

Their father shook his head admiringly. 'It'll be the telly next, you'll see.'

I was anxiously wondering how they were going to get the van back on the track again.

'Everything under control,' Mr Rhys assured me breezily. Now it was empty it wouldn't need much of a push to get it started and on course again.

'What about turning round?'

'No problem. We'll go straight on instead, down the lane past the abbey, on to the main road that way.'

So the venerable Valle Crucis might well be the next obstacle in the path of the wandering pantechnicon. No doubt Mr Rhys would cheerfully claim that, like the barn, the famous ruins could lose a few more stones without it mattering much one way or the other.

Halfway to the gate, Gareth asked if they should put the empty boxes in one of the sheds.

'For the next time you're packing up.'

'Oh, there won't be a next time,' I heard myself say firmly.

'They'll make good kindling then,' Mr Rhys reminded me. '"*Priciau*" we call them in Wales – morning sticks!'

'I won't forget,' I said as I waved them off. Just a few minutes later it was a relief to see the swaying hulk of the van disappear into the dusk, its rear end emblazoned with the farewell logo, 'There Goes Rhys.'

But the day had not yet closed down. Oddly enough, now the rain was over, the air had begun to lighten. Outside the front of the house I stopped in my tracks to watch an extraordinary spectacle taking place, one of these mysterious scene-changes that were to be a regular phenomenon of our life at Hafod. Shape-shifting was the expression that came to mind, the famous ability of the old Welsh wizards to conjure themselves up into different images whenever fate dictated. Behind the hills the veil had been lifted and sunset had taken its place.

Such a sunset, though. The sun itself had gone down but in its wake the whole of the sky at the western end of the valley had become a vast stained-glass window. All the Pre-Raphaelite colours were there, rose and purple, gold and green, as the clouds sank away along the edge of the horizon. Still the light seemed to be expanding in that brilliant afterglow, flickering and pulsing with a life of its own.

In some strange way it seemed to transmit a final charge of energy to the valley itself. Out of nowhere the shape of a hare, ears pricked, went bounding over the field below, and then another. I sat on the wall by the steps to watch them, saw young lambs suddenly running a race to the hedge and swallows streaking and circling out of the barn in pursuit of the last few insects.

Only the mountains were still, that great standing circle surrounding the valley from one end to the other. Their presence was solemn somehow, like the words of a familiar psalm. Just for a moment everything else felt eternal too. I could see the first star tremble above the far chimney, blue woodsmoke drifting down, heady as incense. In that moment it seemed entirely possible to slip away through a chink in time into a different dimension, the secret reality that lay behind the appearance of things.

Then all at once the colours in the sky were gone. New lights appeared, squares of lantern yellow from the farm sheds where milk-churns clanged and a snatch of tenor singing could be heard – Will Davis, no doubt. From the wood behind, the owl chimed in with a hunting call that faded away down the valley.

There was one sound that was constant, though hardly noticed until now. The running of the brook at the bottom of the hill came up clearly in the silence. I wondered why it made me feel at home. Then I remembered that in the islands we had always lived close to the sea. The wash of the waves breaking far out along the reef was endless, a seashell humming in the ear that was part of the air itself.

It seemed the right moment to go inside and finish a piece of work that was urgent. Mopping-up operations and all the other domestic tasks could begin tomorrow. But first there was a writing deadline I had to keep. Fortified with bread and cheese, I lit the oil lamp and brought out my typewriter. The last pages of a book to be published by John Murray had to be posted off within the week. Entitled *A South Sea Spell*, it was a diary of my final Pacific travels, ending up in the kingdom of Tonga.

The great Captain Cook's visits to the island in the 1770s were the counterpoint to my own experiences, especially the accounts of some of his officers on board the expeditionary ships. 'An earthly paradise' was the view of most of them, swept away by the beauty of the islands (and the 'nymphs'), the splendid rituals and dances, and the hedonistic Tongan way of life. In my researches, one Lieutenant David Samwell, a ship's surgeon, had made a special impression on me, writing his letters home with such enthusiasm, as I did two hundred years later.

But where was 'home' for Samwell, I found myself wondering, as I typed out his glowing descriptions? I had one or two reference books in my writing-bag and felt it was time to look him up in some biographical footnotes.

A few lines in small print were instant reward. David Samwell, I learned, was a Welshman, with his own bardic name, Dafydd Ddu Feddyg, or the Doctor in Black. He later became an author in his own right. Originally, though, he came from a village not more than a few miles from Hafod, a village called Nantglyn near Denbigh. His grandfather had been rector of a tiny church at Corwen, even nearer.

So here was an eighteenth-century fellow-traveller who, like me, had left Wales to explore the Pacific and returned eventually to settle in the same idyllic countryside.

I finished the chapter with a flourish. I looked out through the dusty little window at the line of mountains he must have known so well, and said to myself, with Dafydd, 'What the Devil can we wish for more 'til we get to Heaven?'

4

STEPPING-STONES

My first visit to Pen-y-Bryn is always difficult to remember –
not because it was an insignificant event, rather the
opposite. Tea with Megan and Will Davis felt like a landmark
even then, the start of a friendship that was to draw me
into a world I would never otherwise have experienced.

But it blurs in the memory because there were so many
such welcomes into that cluttered farm kitchen with its
slow-ticking clock, a fire stirring in the heart of the shabby
black range whatever the weather. Small rituals repeated
themselves – a dog sent outside for being a nuisance, a curtain
drawn over the door against the draught. Familiar stories
would emerge like stepping-stones out of the fast-running
conversation. It was a flow only occasionally halted by the
search for an elusive English word to match up with the coiled
intricacies of Welsh thinking. And always, there was
something new to talk about, something old to see.

So I'm still not sure. Was this the day Will brought out
the Bronze Age axe-head he'd found while fencing along the
mountain-top? Or was it the time Megan was making
brawn, lifting the lid of the saucepan to show me the pig's
snout bubbling inside? ('Don't worry – Will took out the
eyes for me . . . ') I seem to see two china bowls on the
kitchen table, where the two Sunday cakes were being

mixed, marmalade sponge for Pen-y-Bryn, seed loaf for her sister's family at Pant Glas. The important thing was the wooden spoon, a small worn object which had belonged to her grandmother. No cake would succeed without it. Soon, wiping her hands on her pinny, Megan would be foraging in the bottom cupboard of the second-best dresser, bringing out some battered scrapbook or photograph album she thinks might interest me. All at once time would slip backwards. There were the village children of fifty years ago on their Sunday School outing, stiffly posed in their starched white dresses and collars. There was a solemn muster of quarry workers lined up in dusty black for the funeral of one of the men killed in an explosion. Further on there were ladies in wedding hats, wagons and horses and a splendid steam threshing-machine. And there, seated on the granary steps of Pant Glas, were four generations of the family, from the infant Megan, to the famous Great-Great-Auntie Mair, a pillar of the chapel choir who knew the country spells better than any of the so-called witches of those days, or so said Megan, anyway.

Pant Glas on the other side of the brook was where her sister, Gwyneth, lived. She was married to Will's brother, Owen. 'That was handy, wasn't it?' Megan used to say. The four of them had courted together. Now their 90-year-old mother, known to the young as Nain or Grannie, divided her time between the two homes, 'crossing the water' every six months or so for a change of scene. Pant Glas was the sleepy-looking farm we had passed first on our way up to Hafod, a sprawling old place that boasted some of the original mud and wattle walls and a site that went back to the time of Offa's Dyke.

Pen-y-Bryn had no such picturesque past. Perched on a windy corner of the hill leading down from Hafod, it was a gaunt peaky house armoured against the elements in the grey pebble-dash so loved by the Welsh. On a sunny afternoon it looked almost mellow, I thought, as I wrestled with the binder twine that fastened the old field-gate at the end of the track. Warning barks came up from below and the sheep who had escorted me down melted into the bracken again. Hens scuttled in front of me as I crossed the lane. I had my empty milk-can in my hand, obviously the correct calling card as far as the dogs were concerned. The barking died away and the three of them formed an enthusiastic reception committee around me as I went through into the yard. Snuffles and wags seemed to require some kind of return greeting. To stroke the back of a hard-working sheepdog was to become aware of the driving force of the animal, the wiry framework of bone and muscle so close beneath the black and white fur without an ounce of fat to spare. Pero, Moss and Toss I learned to call them, traditional names in Wales but hard to explain, apart from the fact that *perro* is Spanish for dog, Moss might refer to Moses, and Toss is a useful rhyme. Being related to each other (exactly how I could never remember) there was a strong family resemblance, which could be confusing at first until you remembered the all-important distinctions. Pero had a blue wall-eye. Moss had a boxer's nose – the result of a confrontation with a tractor-wheel. As for Toss, he always reminded me of nothing so much as an old-fashioned Pierrot with the black front of his head shaped like a comedy mask over his thin white face.

All three were Welsh-speaking, of course. A few words from Megan brought them back to order as she came out to greet me. She was smaller and thinner than I remembered from our first encounter, fiftyish and delicate-looking for a farmer's wife.

'You've brought the good weather back with you, anyway.'

Her voice was soft and quick, her face bright with interest as she took the can from me and hung it above the big milk-churn under the porch. We stood together for a moment looking out over the valley with its scattered outposts of farms and cottages. Down below us, Will was enthroned on his tractor with some kind of trailer that raked over the hay as it circled the fields.

'Drying after the rain,' Megan explained. 'He'll be in soon.'

Going in from the back yard, you walked straight into the kitchen. There were boots by the door, grey knobbly socks drying in front of the range (hastily removed by Megan), a kettle steaming on the hob. Something like a discarded hearthrug lay bundled up behind a chair in the corner.

'That's Jethro. He's too old to work now, so he stays inside most of the time. But he sulks a bit.'

Hearing his name, the ancient one raised his head politely and bestowed a toothless smile in my direction. There was the thump of a ragged tail. But he knew better than to follow us into the parlour which was where we had tea on that first visit. Traditional Welshcakes and *bara brith* had been laid out on a lace-edged tray. Willow pattern plates and copper ornaments gleamed against the shelves of the huge oak dresser. There was the righteous smell of old-fashioned wax polish that took me back to my Infants III classroom where we had to shine our desks last thing on a Friday afternoon.

Over tea Megan wanted to know how I had got on last night. She looked concerned. Was I nervous on my own?

'I was fine. I had a fire, slept on the sofa. I was so tired. There's so much to be done up there . . . '

I began to talk about the peeling wallpaper and warped window-frames, the urgent need for electrical power and telephone connection. There seemed to be some trouble with the water too.

'Aye, yes. Trouble with the water . . . '

Will's head had appeared at the parlour door. It was to be a familiar phrase over the years. Hafod and Pen-y-Bryn shared the same water supply which had to travel through a long-buried network of pipes from the well on the hillside half a mile away. This time it seemed the cause of the trouble was sheep, or, rather, one sheep in particular.

'You noticed there was a bit of a blockage then?' Will looked a bit sheepish himself as he sat down on the settle by the door.

'And it was a funny colour too,' I told him.

Will loosened the stud at the top of his collarless shirt. He had brought the sweet-and-sour whiff of work into the parlour together with a touch of carbolic soap.

'Maybe I shouldn't tell you.' He gave me a wink, rubbed the side of his bony nose. 'But when I went up after the old ram yesterday where did I find him but fallen head first into the well! Must have pushed the corrugated iron off, trying to get a drink.'

He caught my expression. 'Don't worry. Can't have been there more than a couple of days. We've put stones on the iron so it shouldn't happen again.'

Megan added her own reassurances. 'The water does get a bit brown sometimes. The peat in the soil, it is, and those old pipes. Best to boil it for a day or two to be on the safe side.'

'You lost a ram then,' I said, to change the subject.

Will laughed. 'He wasn't up to much, that one. Bit past it, I'd say. Be looking out for some new blood soon.'

To my eyes, the rolling tide of sheep that covered the valley all looked roughly the same. Some of the Hafod *habitués* had the initials WD painted in blue on their woolly backsides. But the last month's rain had turned the lettering into the woad-like daubs of Ancient Britons. So how did the owners tell them apart when some went astray?

'It's the ears,' Will said mysteriously.

He beckoned me into the kitchen and opened the drawer of the big scrubbed table. Out of it he brought a battered-looking notebook, bound in black. There was an an air of respect about the way he handled it, turning the pages with careful roughened fingers. All I could see was a series of printed hieroglyphs, interspersed with Welsh names.

'This is a bit private, see.' His voice took on a conspiratorial tone. 'Goes back a long way. Not many outside the valley would know about it.'

Suitably impressed, I felt as if I'd been admitted to some druidical inner circle. Then, as Will went on to explain, the mystery cleared. The hieroglyphs represented the shape of a sheep's ear when it had been clipped in a certain way. Every flock had a different pattern, a series of snips made along the edge of the ear with a small pair of shears. Still today each farmer had his own 'design'. No two were the same, and none was allowed to be copied by another owner.

'Like a Yale key?' I suggested.

Will was amused by this. 'I don't think the old farmers had seen many of *them*.'

'That's the idea, though,' Megan put in encouragingly. She pointed to the rows of names in faded copperplate. 'Every farm is listed in alphabetical order and there's the number of the ear-mark underneath. Like a telephone directory.'

'What about the sheep? Do they mind it?'

There was more amusement at this. It seems the animal hardly reacts apart from a bleat or two. It just gives a shake as if a fly had bitten it and then it is the next one's turn.

Slipping the book back into the drawer, Will brought out something else, a small notepad much scribbled over.

'This is real history, though,' he told me.

Megan made a grab for it. 'Shopping lists. She won't want to see that, Will.'

'What about the stuff on the back?' Will persisted.

Despite herself, Megan began riffling through the pages.

'Only old stories, they are.' She glanced at me shyly. 'Anecdotes, I think you call them. I just write things down when people tell me them. You know.'

I didn't know. But it was then I began to realize that Megan was that rare creature, a natural historian. Her formal education had been scanty. She'd been kept away from the local school by poor health for much of her childhood, she told me later. But the past was her passion. It was something bred in the bone, and every homely detail of it was grist to her mill – the meaning of field names, medieval legends of princes and poets, ghost stories, dog-eared programmes of chapel concerts, notes of Victorian census returns, jotted down on the back of old recipes or seed catalogues, or anything else to hand. As we got to know each other better she would let me see the neatly-written foolscap pages of essays which had won prizes at WI competitions and local eisteddfods. But today it was the shopping notebook that yielded treasure.

'*Cae Goch*,' she mused. 'The Red Field. Plenty of blood spilt in this part of Wales with the English always after our land, trying to get the better of us.' She tucked a pair of crooked specs onto the end of her nose and screwed up her eyes to focus on the tiny scribble. 'The Place of the She-Bear, though. That's Dafydd's field higher up. Now where does that name come from, I wonder?'

'Back to the days when there were bears in the forests,' I suggested.

But Megan was onto the next page. 'And then there's the Field of Graves. I know about that one, down by the river.' She gave a little shiver. 'Auntie Mair used to tell me the English soldiers had been buried in their armour. I used to dream about that when I was little, thinking about all those ghosts clanking up through the trees on a moonlight night.'

We were brought back to reality by the sound of the telephone, a muffled trill from the passageway where it hung on the wall, shrouded by coats. While Will went to answer it, I remembered I had to make some urgent calls. I listed them to Megan – the electricity people, a carpenter, a plumber, an engineer for the disabled phone.

Nodding briskly, Megan ticked them off on her fingers.

'So you'll want Sammy Sparks from Llangollen. And Jack Williams down at the old quarry. Then Will's cousin, Morgan, can do all kinds of jobs especially plumbing.' She put the notebook back in the drawer and got to her feet. 'I'll ring them for you if you like.'

'Be quicker that way,' said Will, back in the kitchen with two more cups of tea.

She disappeared into the passage, but she was back again the next minute, doubled up with laughter, her hand clapped over her mouth.

'What did I do? After all that talk about sheep – '

'What then?' asked Will, feigning exasperation.

'Dialled the number of Morgan's sheep-mark instead of the house!'

Will rolled his eyes to the ceiling. 'Wonder you didn't get to talk to some of his sheep!'

Megan fled back to the phone, still giggling to herself.

It seemed that cousin Morgan was a busy farmer, in between sorting out the local plumbing problems. 'We all do a bit of everything up here,' said Will. 'Have to, don't we?'

There was a pause in the conversation as he brought out a tin of tobacco and got to work on his pipe. In the background I could hear Megan talking in Welsh with the occasional dash of English. I gathered that 'Hafod' was what I was being called, as in 'Hafod's here for the milk' or 'Hafod needs the electric on'. It was a Welsh habit, also an ingenious way of avoiding the formality of surnames while we were still getting to know each other. I liked the sound of it too. Hearing myself called by the name of my house touched a proprietorial chord somehow, made me feel that I had become part of a vanishing breed of true mountain dwellers.

Afterwards I made a reverse charge phone call to R in London, cramming into a few minutes an account of life at Hafod so far, not an easy task. Yes, all was well, I told him, and I was looking forward to his arrival on the scene next week. Meanwhile work on the house would be starting right away, thanks to the Davises.

'You'll be glad to have your husband up there,' Megan said. 'And family too?'

As soon as the holidays began, I told her, no doubt with equally enthusiastic friends in tow.

We were standing out by the gate now.

'We have no children,' Megan told me. 'But plenty of family,' she added quickly. Her third sister, Bethan, had half a dozen children, some of them growing up already to start work on their own farm close to the village. 'And all our friends' – she swept a hand around the valley and beyond – 'everyone joins in to help at times like shearing, or getting in the hay.'

'And gathering the mountain,' said Will, who was leaning on the gate to smoke the last of his pipe.

Gathering the mountain. It was a fine expression, I thought, though I had no idea what it meant. Apparently it is the task of bringing the sheep down onto lower ground for the winter. Dogs and men go up in force. Every rock and peak has to be searched for the last runaway to be rounded up.

'The hardest day's work of the year,' Will pronounced it. He pointed to the great bulwark of limestone cliffs that encircled the far end of the valley. 'Especially when we have to get round some of those nooks and crannies.'

It was a famous landmark, rising up in tiers like a ruined amphitheatre. The slanting sun of late afternoon turned the limestone into quartz, with shimmering highlights of silver and rose. 'Worlds End', the sign-post said at the end of the lane, catching the eerie strangeness of the spectacle. But the Eglwyseg is its historical name. It has no exact translation and yet the Welsh word for a church – Eglwys – is embedded in it like some mysterious fossil. Ancient burial caves are supposed to be hidden deep in the rocks. No archaeologist has seriously investigated this claim, but locally each outcrop has a legend of its own, it seems.

'Arthur's Seat, Maiden's Leap,' Megan recited dreamily. 'I've written a sort of Eglwyseg play for the WI to do at Christmas,' she went on, animated now, her pale cheeks suddenly pink. 'Say half a dozen members representing the different peaks, telling the tales about them.'

Will gave a little snort. 'Who's to be the big one at the

top? Supposed to be a giantess up there, wasn't there, keeping guard against invaders?'

'That'll be Menna,' Megan said firmly. 'She can be standing on a chair at the back.'

'Won't need a chair,' Will murmured. Grinning to himself, he pulled on his cap. 'What it is to have a creative wife,' were his parting words, said with a touch of pride as he set off back to the field.

It was time I was getting back to Hafod. Megan ladled out a canful of milk from the churn for me, then put a bag with half a dozen eggs and a fresh loaf of bread into my other hand.

'Keep you going until you can go shopping. Will can give you a lift into town any time.'

What about the bus, I asked? The estate agents had made enthusiastic mention of local transport and I was eager to sample it.

Tuesday morning ten o'clock from the village was the timetable, it seemed. 'Back again in the afternoon,' she added cheerfully. She popped a red geranium plant into the top of the bag.

'Be nice in the kitchen window when the winter comes.'

It was hard to imagine winter as I walked up the lane with the sun on my back. The dogs came with me for part of the way, chasing each other in and out of the hedges, until they were summoned back with a whistle from Will. The air was rich with the scent of hay and the foxgloves stood in purple ranks on either side of the track. It was quite a climb up to the first little side-gate to Hafod. Everywhere the bracken was waist-high, for as far up as the blue of the sky above the mountain. All around Hafod itself a thick tangle of hawthorn and hazel and elder trees was forcing its way through the wire fencing, uprooting the edge of the bottom wall. We would have to add a stone-mason to the rest of the list, I thought, when I was next at Pen-y-Bryn.

I sat down on the bench at the top of the path and decided it was far too beautiful a day to go indoors just yet.

Besides, I had spent the morning industriously mopping and scrubbing, hadn't I? Amongst the rioting greenery I could see the pink of a smothered rose-bush or two, and some six-foot-high yellow wallflowers in a languorously scented wilderness of their own. Something made me remember the Fijian cane-knife I had found at the bottom of one of the crates, a hefty broad-bladed affair used in the islands to harvest the sugar. Tuki the gardener had made good use of it to keep down the undergrowth in our garden at Lautoka. When we were packing up he handed it to me wrapped in a page of the *Fiji Times*. It would be a good thing to take home with us, he said. No doubt he envisaged Wales as a savage kind of country, overrun with dangerous jungle.

He wasn't far wrong either, I thought as I armed myself to hack my way through stinging nettles and thorn-laden brambles. After an hour, no less than twenty steps had emerged, some of stone, some of wood, winding their way up the bank behind the house. Drugged bumble-bees were stumbling out of some forgotten snapdragons. Overhead a flock of butterflies, Peacocks, Admirals and anonymous whites, were weighing down the branches of a wild Buddleia that smelt overpoweringly of honey. Suddenly exhausted, I collapsed on a tree-stump by the gate. To my surprise, a stranger was sitting nearby, a grey squat figure, waiting for the dusk, or perhaps a refreshing shower.

'Good old Toad,' I said, reverting to *Wind in the Willows* language in my pleasure at this encounter. Like the owl in the privy he was a much older inhabitant than I was and I felt his presence was to be respected. Then, with a blink, he shuffled away into a hole at the bottom of the tree-trunk, obviously his private hermitage. I must remember not to disturb his dandelion garden, next time I come round with my cane-knife, I thought.

Back at the house the rooms inside felt free from the smell of damp for the first time. The doors and windows had been open, and the air was warm and fresh. Tomorrow there would be callers and the place would slowly acquire that indefinable lived-in feeling which was something I passionately wanted for it.

Before I went in, I stood in the porch for a moment, looking down at Pen-y-Bryn in the distance. The hay-meadow was quiet, the tractor standing idle at the bottom of the slope, with Will no doubt inside the house having his supper. But the field itself was a wonderful sight. The cut grass had been combed flat by the trailer making a perfect pattern of concentric circles, spiralling outwards like ripples on a lake. Tomorrow it would disappear as if it had never been. A new machine would come to parcel up the hay into stacks and the field would be busy with the figures of Will and his helpers, children playing, the dogs barking around the wagons. That was another picture, a traditional rural scene from so many paintings of the past. But, at this moment, it was an even older landscape, one of magic and silence, as if the curving lines had been drawn as part of a harvest spell, waiting for the moon to come up.

Outside the porch a large moth blundered by. I went inside and closed the door. It was time to light the lamps.

5

PRESIDING SPIRITS

In my mind's eye, I always see the shape of Wales on the map as an enclosed and separate place. It has turned its back on the rest of the country, a craggy profile jutting out westwards, looking firmly to the sea. The boundary with England runs down behind it as clear-cut as the invisible line I used to imagine as a child. If a giant's scissors descended on it, or a fault in the earth opened up, we would float away, free as an island.

In the eighteenth century, this idea of separateness was the chief fascination of Wales as far as travellers from England were concerned. For the adventurous patrons of the fashionable 'Welch Tour' it was an awesome experience to make the crossing into unknown territory where the sheer scale of the 'rude and horrid' peaks and ravines defied the imagination and the peasant inhabitants communicated in an uncouth language of their own. Druidical descendants of the Ancient Britons was how the visiting poets saw them. Driven to this last stronghold by the barbarian hordes, they were upholders of 'true mountain Liberty', guardians of Snowdon's sacred spring, according to the youthful Shelley, in his 1812 poem, *On Leaving London for Wales*.

This romantic view of splendid isolation may be lost in the past, the product of overwrought English sensibilities. But to us Welsh, the sense of a different identity is real enough, as it always has been. The sound of a living language reminds you if it every day. So do the political overtones of independence. For me, though, it's something much more personal and more subtle. To wake at Hafod is to know you are in 'another country' before you even open your eyes. The air of Wales carries its own special messages I think as I lie in bed, still half-asleep. In Wales you have different dreams, darker and more mysterious. Even as these fade, there's a kind of tribal reassurance at finding yourself in a place where you belong.

In the half-light the house is enfolded in the peculiar dense silence of the mountains. There is always an underlying hum about it though, very faint, as if some subterranean psychic energy is at work, keeping us slowly turning from one season to the next. Perhaps it comes from the Bronze Age bones deep in the ground, or those magnetic ley lines running between the ancient look-out points and the standing stones of Eglwyseg. Whatever its secrets, I like to think my mountain has a presiding spirit and consider myself lucky to be living in its shadow.

Now I'm awake, other messages start to surface. If it's been raining, the moist earthy smell from outside breathes through every crack and cranny. There might even be a drop or two hanging from the corner of the ceiling where there are signs of a leak from the gable end. If it's windy there's that click of a loose frame in the little window at the back, also a sort of sepulchral sighing from the closed-up chimney behind the wall. The squirrels have started up a tap-dance on the slates overhead, bringing down nuts from the hazel trees. And whatever the weather there is the blackbird who sings in Welsh, showing off all his tenor trills and counter-melodies.

This was the way the morning announced itself at Hafod, right from the start. That first week, however, I was up in good time, on the alert for the arrival of the promised army of helpers. The early sun was warm in the doorway, and Will and his friends were already busy in the fields below. In the distance, children's voices flew back and forth like arrows.

No sign of anything coming along the road through, unless you counted a small red beetle crawling out of the greenery, down by the brook.

Ten minutes later the beetle had been transformed into a mail van, parked at the gate. I had forgotten about the post, hardly believing there would be a personal delivery so far off the beaten track. But here coming up the path was a proper postman in neat navy blue. He was carrying a cardboard box.

'*Bore da!*'

'Good morning!'

I was hovering in the porch, still in my dressing-gown, eager to see what was being delivered.

'No mail today,' he called. 'But I've got an owl for you.'

'An owl?' Did postmen in Wales often bring birds instead of letters?

This postman had a knowing grin and a gypsy's black moustache.

'Tell you what happened,' he said, collapsing breathless onto the bench. My attention was fixed on the box. The lid was half-open but all that could be seen was a ruffled tawny shape, crouched at the bottom like a wary cat. Apparently Ollie – the name of the owl not the postman – had been found injured on the roadside a few days ago. On impulse, Dewi – as the postman introduced himself – took him home to recover. The vet mended the fractured wing and said he would soon be able to fly again. But Ollie seemed reluctant to follow this advice.

'Only confidence he needs, see. Trouble is,' Dewi went on – 'he's been making a bit of a mess of the spare room and the wife's mother's coming to stay next week. So – '

'We've got an owl already,' I interrupted, somewhat irrationally.

'He'll be no trouble.' Dewi's voice became ever more undulating in his mission to persuade. 'I'll fix him up on a perch up a tree. Somewhere in the wilds he should be, not where we live in Market Street. I heard people had moved into Hafod so I said to myself I'll see if they won't mind Ollie trying his wings on the mountain.'

I peered into the box. A pair of enormous eyes blinked back at me.

'Shall I have a look at him then?' I said, weakening.

'I'll bring him into the kitchen. Perhaps time for a *paned?*'

It was hard to concentrate on our mugs of tea at the kitchen table with Ollie perched on the back of the chair next to me. He seemed to be wobbling a bit in this position.

'He likes a broomhandle best,' Dewi explained.

The yard brush was arranged across two chairs and from here Ollie settled down to survey his surroundings. He seemed quite relaxed as Dewi stroked his back. Never having entertained an owl before, I studied him as closely as I could without being impolite. The rich brown plumage was artistically speckled and shaded. I was also struck by his ability to swivel his huge head in what seemed like a complete circle, turning his gaze from one to the other of us as we talked. The eyelids were a delicate dark-blue with curling lashes that gave him a distinctly theatrical look.

'What does he eat?' I whispered. For some reason, one lowers one's voice in the presence of an owl, especially a convalescent owl. So far the beak had remained firmly closed against the fragments of toast and marmalade on offer. Apparently raw meat was his preferred diet, fresh mice being in short supply in Dewi's household. Dewi had brought a piece of steak with him, also a home-made perch shaped like a sentry-box. Within minutes he had climbed halfway up a fir tree with it and Ollie was installed inside with his breakfast.

'Don't worry about him,' was Dewi's parting cry. 'Be back again tomorrow. He'll have taken off by then, you'll see.'

From time to time I was able to glimpse a shadowy form standing guard inside the box, but nothing more. Luckily around mid-morning I was distracted by another caller, otherwise the whole day would have been spent checking up on Ollie.

With the arrival of Sam Thomas, though, I had to pull myself together. Sammy Sparks was the perfect name for him, I thought, this wiry elfin figure in a bobble hat who seemed to crackle with energy as he sprang to and fro round the tangled network of Hafod's 'electricals'.

'Lucky I know the old place, isn't it?' he called down from his ladder outside the back door. 'Not many would think of looking for a fuse-box in the *ty bach*.'

I agreed. An outside privy was not the usual place for this vital piece of equipment. It seemed that Sammy had been looking after Hafod's mod cons ever since the days of the much-vaunted generator.

'Under the steps by the gate it was. Had to give it a good kick to get it going too, the old bugger, especially in cold weather. So the ladies needed a bit of help with it, I can tell you.'

By now Sammy was back in the house darting hither and thither to check up on the wiring. This had been added to over the years so that it looped along in spaghetti-like strands over doorways, down walls, under beams, and anywhere else it was possible to make a connection, however tenuous. The general effect was of some kind of permanent Christmas decorations. All seemed to be in working order though apart from one forlorn flex hanging from the ceiling of the so-called study, which gave up the ghost in a splutter of blue smoke.

I assured Sammy that I wasn't too keen on overhead lights anyway, especially if there was a fire hazard.

Sammy nodded. When he was up again he'd put in some extra lamp sockets for me.

'Talking about fires though . . . ' he went on. Work over, we were sitting at the dining-room table where I'd been unpacking a few stray bottles out of the last of the boxes. Sammy raised his glass of sherry to propose a toast to the new owners of Hafod and was now embarked on his childhood memories of the war. The night the German planes had dropped bombs on the mountains was enshrined in local legend. Oil drums had been set alight on the moors as flares to deceive the pilots into thinking they were over the Liverpool munitions factories.

'So what with the bombs and the decoys there was one hell of a fire up there,' was how Sammy put it.

This produces a flash-back of my own – Wrexham station full of smoke from the mountain and the exciting smell of burning the day we arrived back from our annual seaside holiday. As the GWR train steams in, adding to the confusion, the tiny figure of my grandmother, Jenny Ellis, comes rushing down the platform to meet us. She is wearing her best black and waving her umbrella, her high-pitched voice more Welsh than usual.

'The Germans are bombing us! You must take the children back to Pwllheli!'

No such luck, I remember thinking. Sure enough, I was back in my navy-blue gymslip and panama the very next day while the famous fire dwindled into a cloud on the horizon as far as Wrexham was concerned.

Not for Sammy, though. His family had a farm on the mountainside and even now he could see their big shire horse lying in the grass next morning with six pieces of shrapnel through his chest.

'Only animals had been the casualties, they told us. Poor old Colonel, though. Standing in the field one minute, dead the next. Nearly broke my heart, it did.'

Sammy's eyes dimmed for a moment, then brightened again.

'What about the barrage balloon though? That was the real excitement for us kids – there were fifteen of us, remember. It had got loose from Liverpool and one day there was this great big elephant sailing over the house. Next thing the cables got caught on the roof, pulled the chimney off and then the whole thing came down on the bottom field. The sheep didn't like it, I can tell you. All those bits of burning rubber dropping onto them out of the blue. And just after shearing too!'

It was the chimney that most upset his father, though. Such a fine old house it was, nothing had changed there for centuries. With that Welsh gift for making pictures, Sammy conjured up room after room for me as he talked – the blue slab floors in the best kitchen, the hiding cupboards under the stairs, the oak panels in the parlour. The place was always full of people. Every harvest, the big bread oven was packed with loaves and roasting beef for the men in the fields.

Carried away now, he sprang to his feet, demonstrating with outstretched arms the size of the basement dairy where the butter was churned and the 'ice-cold' larder cut into the bank and lined with slate. At the back steps there was still the rail for dismounting, with a date carved above the door, 1727.

'Long before that, though, it was some kind of hostelry, they say. On the main road, see. The Pilgrims' Path it was called then, back in the Middle Ages.'

Sammy paused for breath. For a few moments we'd both been away somewhere else, back in the past which always in Wales seems to be mysteriously interlocked with the present. Then came the melancholy end to his account. The family gone, Sammy in bachelor quarters in town, the old house had stood empty for years.

'"Trespassers Will Be Prosecuted,"' he quoted wryly. 'Until the council decide what to do with it. The Welsh name means The Most Favoured Place. And that's just what it was.'

He sighed, looked at the grandfather clock that didn't work, and then at his watch. He still had another place to call at, seven miles away in the next valley. The phone was working now anyway and next time he'd be up with a cooker and a fridge. He knew just where to lay his hands on them. No point in getting new, was there?

Hurrying away with his bag of tools, he was his practical everyday self again. But in my imagination I was still stranded somewhere between the Middle Ages and the last war. Why was it, I found myself wondering, that every encounter in this part of the world led on to a totally unexpected scenario? Even the last line took me by surprise, as he reappeared at the window.

'Do you like sloe gin then?'

'I think so.'

'The tree by the gate's full of them. Plenty of sugar and a pint of the Gordons and I'll do you a bottle for Christmas.' He winked at me. '"Sammy's Special" they call it. That'll get you through the winter all right.'

Off once again, he stopped in his tracks to greet another caller.

'Here comes old Si,' he reported. 'Make sure he gets your measurements right!'

I was still puzzling over this quip as Mr Silas Jenkins introduced himself as the promised carpenter. He'd been sent by his brother-in-law, Morgan, the one who was a cousin of Will Davis. A pale, quietly-spoken person he went to work examining the window-frames and measuring for extra cupboards and shelves, without much comment. The air of discreet expertise with which he wielded the tape-measure impressed me particularly.

'I expect you've seen my place in the town,' he said at one point. 'You've probably noticed the memorials.'

I explained that I hadn't yet explored the town properly. Meanwhile my brain was juggling with 'memorials'. Enlightenment came when he brought out his order-book to jot down the necessary particulars. There at the top was the heading, 'Jenkins and Son Undertakers and Stonemasons'. 'Builders and Carpenters' was in smaller print underneath. 'No Job Too Small.'

Presumably sixty-something Silas was the 'And Son' of this multi-talented business. Like Sammy Sparks, it seemed he too had a long acquaintance with Hafod, carrying out various 'improvements' for the Misses Sinclair, most of which seemed to focus on the need to economize on electricity. Extra daylight was the ladies' command. With amazing ingenuity, father and son had slotted in a series of surprise windows in the most unlikely places, so that one came across chinks of frosted glass where least expected, up the stairs and under the stairs, high up in the parlour wall looking out on the back passageway, even in the little lean-to where the boiler was installed. Bookshelves too were constantly being commissioned.

'Great readers they were – '

The sealing up of mouse-holes in the bedrooms was a minor operation but equally important.

'They tried to do it with old stockings but the mice only used them for nests.' Mr Jenkins told me. 'And they did enjoy eating chocolates in bed – the ladies, not the mice,' he added with something like a smile.

Humming a hymn-tune under his breath, he neatly fastened up his box of tools. All the time my mind was returning to coffins and Rhys the Remove's remark on the narrowness of the stairs.

With the sensitivity of his profession, Mr Jenkins seemed to be reading my thoughts. The eldest sister had passed away peacefully in her bed some years ago, he confided. He and his father had made all the arrangements and the stairs were managed with some success. The real problem was the weather. It was the middle of one of the worst winters for years and the snow on the track was so deep that not even a car could get through to the house, let alone a hearse. So in the end it was Will Davis and his tractor who came to the rescue and got the coffin safely down to the road for the funeral in the village.

'I'm not so sure old Miss Lottie would have liked that,' he said in the doorway. 'She was a bit of a stickler for tradition.'

We both looked down the track, imagining the scene. Somehow I could see it more clearly than many a summer picture – the little coffin perched at the back of the old red tractor, the dogs in attendance on either side, the line of mourners trudging behind, black against the snow.

I listened out for the sound of Ollie that night. I could hear our resident owl making his usual circuit of the Hafod wood. But under the fir-tree all was silent. Shining my torch up through the branches, I had a feeling that the sentry-box was empty. No doubt the visitor had gone in search of a property he could call his own.

Nor did I see him again. In the morning, however, I discovered that he had not left without a farewell feast to sustain him. On the ground beneath the tree were the remains of his night's hunting – the wings of a very small magpie, with the severed feet laid side by side as neatly as a pair of shoes outside a hotel bedroom.

6

ON THE WHY-WALK BUS

Tuesday morning. Time to catch the one and only bus into town to buy food. Time to set out on the expedition down one side of the valley and up the next to reach the road from the village where the bus would stop. If I was there, of course.

At one point I wasn't at all sure I would be. After days spent on domestic tasks, a walk was something of a novelty, especially one taken at an angle of approximately forty-five degrees. But round the last bend up the last hill, Pant Glas farm appeared, home of Megan's sister and their mother, Mrs Roberts. So help was at hand if needed. Shamefully winded, I collapsed onto a stone marker on the bank to get some of my breath back before the final lap to the top. From here I could see someone outside the front porch – a white-haired old lady enthroned on a kitchen chair. Framed by hollyhocks and an archway of honeysuckle, a lavender-coloured shawl round her shoulders, she looked the perfect image of Victorian rural tranquillity as she sat dozing in the sun.

'All right, are you?' came a piercing voice.

Mrs Roberts was, in fact, sharply wide awake.

Stick in hand, she made her way briskly across the yard to take a better look at me. Behind her glasses, her blue eyes were bright as marbles, every wrinkle in her face quivering with curiosity.

'Hafod, isn't it?'

'And you must be Megan's mother,' I said.

Even at the time I realized it was hardly an adequate title for this venerable icon of Welsh life, landowner and law-maker, famous matriarch of a numberless tribe of Roberts relations and descendants scattered from one end of the valley to the other, and beyond.

Women in Wales are not given to shaking hands. Mrs Roberts reached out over the gate to bestow an encouraging pat instead. Settling her shawl over her shoulders, she was now ready for a chat. Alas, this was not the moment for a proper conversation.

'I'm on my way to catch the bus,' I explained.

'Of course.' She nodded graciously. 'You must come in next time when Gwyneth's here.' She peered up at the white blob on the opposite mountain. 'Hafod,' she mused. 'All sorts used to live up there in the old days.'

'What sorts would those be, Mrs Roberts?'

Five minutes to go. I mustn't miss the bus, but I didn't want to miss this either.

'Well, I was only little. But the ones I remember best were a quarry worker called Ned with his family at one end, and Mr Parry, the old gamekeeper, at the other. A deacon he was, too, a very respectable man. Different as chalk from cheese they were. You could tell that just from hearing them walk past the house on their way home.' Glancing round at a circle of phantom eavesdroppers, the old lady lowered her voice. 'On a Sunday evening it would be Mr and Mrs Parry singing a bit of a hymn together, after chapel. But on Fridays, there'd be Ned and his wife, fighting and cursing cat-and-dog after a night on the drink at The Sun Inn down the road. Most of his wage packet gone too, I expect. My mother used to close my bedroom window when she heard them coming.'

I laughed. 'I hope they won't start keeping us awake at Hafod.'

As I turned to go, Mrs Roberts pointed down to the river.

'There goes the old heron. Flying upstream today so there's rain to come later. Got your umbrella though, I see.'

There was no time for more than a glimpse of a solemn shape, flapping slowly along the water's edge. In the distance a small blue bus had appeared on the road from the village.

'Don't rush yourself, *cariad*,' Mrs Roberts called after me. 'Trevor will wait for you.'

Which indeed he did, merely shaking his bald head in mock rebuke as I climbed aboard, still out of breath. Among the cheerful cargo of women shoppers silence had fallen, followed by a low buzz of speculation. As ever, I heard the name Hafod being passed helpfully around. Country faces watched and waited while I fished in my purse for the required ten pence. Then with a wild lurch, the bus started up again and I found myself deposited in the lap of a chubby-faced lady in a Fair Isle jumper.

'Not to worry,' she assured me, settling me into the seat next to her. 'You're all right.' As she picked up my basket and umbrella, clucking and smiling, it was evident she had taken me under her wing. Behind us there seemed to be a general consensus of opinion that the new arrival would indeed be 'all right' with Gwen.

'Gwen'll show you the ropes,' said someone with a warning chortle.

'Have you into the WI before you can blink,' another voice added.

'I'm Gwen Price,' said my friend, adding for identification, 'Price, Pandy Farm, the other side from the village. Lucky it's the WI market in town today so you'll be able to get a home-made sponge at least. Do you know the shops at all?'

Without waiting for an answer, she ran through a recommended list, Watkin the butchers, Ellis greengrocers, Myfanwy at the bakery, as well as the whereabouts of chemist and post office, adding, as an afterthought, that Mr Humphreys, the grocer, might even deliver if he took a fancy to me.

I made a mental note of this. 'Llangollen sounds bigger than I thought,' I said.

Gwen was quick to reassure me. 'No, no. Only one main street and a few little ones. It's changed a bit though, like the valley. There don't seem to be the characters around these days, somehow.'

'The old-timers are dropping off, it is,' a small, whiskery man complained from a few seats back. In fact, now I looked more closely, there were two of them, subdued figures in flat caps, tucked away amongst the overflowing female contingent.

'Like old Willie Why-Walk,' piped his companion. 'The one who started the first bus in the valley.'

'"Why Walk"?' I repeated. I waited for the obligatory punchline. It came in a positive chorus.

'"Why-Walk-When-We're-Running"!'

'That was his slogan, see,' someone explained. 'Willie was a character all right.'

There was a grinding of brakes as we slewed round a hairpin bend into a side lane that ran across the next valley.

'Bit of a Stirling Moss is Trevor,' Gwen told me *sotto voce*. 'Likes to hit the accelerator so's we can have extra shopping time he says. He's in a hurry for rehearsal today, though. The Male Voice are doing *Nabucco* next week.'

More grinding followed while we manoeuvred a risky dip in the track. The cardboard box by Trevor's feet became strangely agitated. From under the lid a strangled cry could be heard. For a moment I thought Ollie had decided to make a return trip into town.

'That's Maggie's prize hen,' the lady behind told us. 'She's sending it to her sister at Rhewl. Dilys's haven't been laying properly for weeks.'

'I should think all Maggie's are prize hens,' said Gwen. 'The way she has them in and out of the house like cats. Gwilym went there once delivering cattle-feed and they were scratching around on the kitchen table, if you like. Said it put him right off his cup of tea.'

A RAM IN THE WELL

All the time the picture postcard scenery was streaming past the window unremarked. Foaming waterfalls dashed beneath hump-backed bridges. Vistas of blue mountain slopes rose and fell through lush green forests. Along the lanes whitewashed cottages stood deep in dog-daisies, with milk-churns waiting in the shade. Every now and then there was a halt by the wayside, heralded by a warning shout from the back.

'Mrs Morgan gets off here, Trevor. Saves her walking.'

Then, 'Hold on, there's Mr Edwards just coming through the gate for you.'

'Knowledge Edwards, that is,' Gwen told me when the elderly man in a black jacket had made his way to his seat, a bulging haversack over his shoulder. 'Used to be schoolmaster at Llangarw. Got more facts in his head than the *Encyclopaedia Britannica*, and he still goes down to the library for his books, regular as clockwork.'

Half a mile further on someone else was waiting by the road, a wild-looking figure who sprang forward waving what looked like a guard's flag as the bus came into sight. But Trevor simply sped past with a friendly nod.

'Not stopping?' I asked him, wondering why.

'No need,' he told me, over his shoulder. 'It's only old Crad.'

Old Crad was there most days, it seemed, on the look-out for passing vehicles. Not quite right in the head, as everyone hastened to explain.

'Not since he retired from the railway.'

'Lives with his sister by the crossing-gates.'

'No harm to anyone, is he, poor dab?'

Now we were back on the main road again. Ahead of us appeared the rooftops of Llangollen, encircled by hills, the remains of Dinas Brân Castle hunchbacked against the clouds. Down below the River Dee flung itself over the rocks, swirling in Merlinesque torrents between the arches of the bridge that was one of the Seven Wonders of Wales (reverently recited by us as children). As we roared across into town this operatic scenario was enhanced by Trevor's practice run of the Anvil chorus, his throbbing baritone-bass punctuated by grace notes on the horn. With a final flourish, we drew up in a side-street alongside the Toiledau Merched (Ladies Convenience).

It had already begun to dawn on me that the threatened dearth of local characters was an illusion. Even now, there was this striking lady in white gloves and floral two-piece who appeared from the back of the bus to lead us all off. Long earrings swung beneath a rolled-up hairdo that was a rather richer black than nature had intended as she went by in a drift of eau-de-Cologne. The usual smiles and good mornings were exchanged with the other passengers. Only a little old woman sitting bolt upright at the side refused to join in.

'I don't know you,' I heard her announce.

The words popped out through buttoned-up lips. But the lady in gloves was not dismayed.

'Ah, you must be a visitor then,' she replied, airily disappearing down the steps with a regal wave.

Was I the only person to be startled by this exchange, I wondered afterwards, or was it just the usual hint of Welsh scandal seething beneath the surface of everyday life? At any rate, the subject was obviously taboo for a newcomer like myself.

'Buried three husbands, that one,' was all Gwen said, as the vision disappeared in the direction of The Harp and Goat.

7

A Bargain from Benny the Bid

Emerging from the Why-Walk into the heart of Llangollen, I was glad to have Gwen with me. After the cloistered calm of Hafod it was like being dropped into Oxford Circus on a Saturday afternoon, except that everyone seemed to know everyone else. Traffic jams sweated and fumed in the narrow High Street, between pavements that were crammed with country shoppers. At every corner long-lost friends and relations were greeting each other in bilingual floods of gossip and news, while rough dogs from the farms struck up wary liaisons in shop doorways. A rich smell of meat pies wafted out from under the butchers' awnings. 'Genuine Welsh Oggies' read the mysterious label on the trays of gigantic pasties. Standing in front of the window, an American lady tourist, dressed for the beach, was repeating the legend to the rest of the party.

'Well, fancy that! Maybe we should try them.'

We were making for the WI market which was tucked away in the old Town Hall, a small Gothic edifice next to a frowning chapel. Once inside there was a strong aroma of municipal dignity about the polished oak fittings and the newly-washed Victorian tiles. As we climbed the stairs, the town clock struck a stately midday chime.

'Time for refreshments,' Gwen declared.

Inside the room at the top, trestle counters were thronged with helpers and buyers. According to Gwen, though, the 'locusts' had already been and gone, leaving nothing much behind. There was enough at least to put into my basket the last lemon sponge, a pot of rhubarb and ginger jam and a home-made *bara brith*, also a weedy-looking mint cutting, which, it was agreed, looked a bit *digalon* – that useful Welsh expression for anything down-hearted, plants included. Gwen said it would spread like wild-fire at Hafod and make all the difference to our Sunday lamb.

A flurry of introductions accompanied these purchases deftly managed by Gwen, before we retreated to a corner table with our coffee and sandwiches. It was a bit like sitting in the wings of an old-fashioned music-hall. Amongst other things, the Town Hall was also the heart of Llangollen's theatreland, it seemed. Maroon velvet curtains were swathed around a stage that was already set for some forthcoming production with a backdrop of elves and fairies and giant toadstools. At present the magic forest was occupied by WI committee members counting out the morning's proceeds but, with the footlights gleaming, the local orchestra tuning up and the balcony packed with encouraging faces, I could well imagine the first night of *A Midsummer Night's Dream* or *The Sound of Music*. According to Gwen, the wildly flourishing Operatic Society also had to compete with half a dozen drama clubs as well as the Christmas pantomime season which enrolled the entire population of under-tens into the cast and ran for weeks.

'What about the International Eisteddfod?' I asked. I'd been trying to imagine the ethnic multitudes of drummers and dancers from all round the world packing themselves onto the boards of the Town Hall for this famous *fiesta*.

'Oh no!' Gwen laughed. 'They need a whole field to

themselves, tents and marquees, the lot. Dancing in the streets as well, if it's fine. You'll be here to see it for yourself next year anyway, won't you?' She looked at me quizzically. 'I mean, is it true you are settling into Hafod permanently?'

Permanently, I assured her. I was thinking of the moment the big iron key turned in the back door and the first smoke floated up from the far chimney – as well as my ongoing campaigns against mice and mildew and constipated water-pipes.

'In that case – '

Gwen took the kind of deep breath that precedes an important decision. She hadn't talked about it on the bus, she said, as people round here were only too nosy about everyone else's business. But, in fact, Hafod was a house that had become part of her own life over the years.

'It was the Miss Sinclairs, you see. They needed a bit of help with the old place, so once a week I'd walk over from the farm to give them a hand.'

The arrangement had started off with some wallpapering, moved on to the brasses and the beeswax and ended up with keeping the whole place in order. The ladies themselves needed a bit of watching too.

'Like the time I found them fast asleep in what they called the sun-lounge. Knocked out they were by the fumes from that Vapona thing they'd hung up against the flies. What would have happened if it hadn't been one of my Thursdays, I often ask myself?'

'What indeed?' I murmured. I began to think that a renewal of Gwen's weekly visits could prove something of an insurance policy.

'Of course you're only half their age,' she added, shooting me another of her shrewd glances. 'But if you ever needed a bit of help . . . '

As a result of this conversation Thursdays thereafter were never just an ordinary day of the week. This was chiefly because Gwen was no ordinary person. At that point, I couldn't say why exactly. But there was just a clue to the mystery as we left.

'I suppose you thought I was as Welsh as everyone else on that bus,' she said suddenly, sounding more Welsh than ever with the catchy see-saw inflexion of the north. The shiny cheeks, the curly black hair and the sense of zest about her, could only be country Celt, a perfect example of the down-to-earth hill farmer's wife. And yet –

'Well, don't be deceived!' she broke in, laughing. 'A mistress of disguise is what I am. Or camouflage, more like. The first thing my father-in-law said to me was, "You're a foreigner, aren't you?" Almost the last thing too!'

We were standing out on the pavement together. 'Time to tell you about that when I come up to Hafod,' she said. 'It'll be lovely to see the place again. Gets a real hold of you, somehow, doesn't it?'

Then she was off, bustling purposefully through the shoppers to meet her husband at the cattle-market.

'Gets a hold of you' was exactly the right expression for Hafod, I thought. I'd been in its grip from the very first day. Even now, after just an hour or so away from the place, I was beginning to feel homesick. The Why-Walk was due to make the return journey at two o'clock – all being well with Trevor's rehearsal. So now I must concentrate on my shopping.

It wasn't much of a problem, in fact. Wherever I went the decisions were already made for me. The butchers meant local lamb chops, with an exuberant Mr W W, cheerfully bloodstained at his marble altar, dispensing expert advice amongst the hanging carcases, with sawdust on the floor and a bentwood chair for chatty customers. A visit to Ellis Greengrocer – maybe a distant relative of mine to judge from the saturnine profile – produced a bag of best leeks, field mushrooms, 'our own potatoes' and, as a sideline, a pair of Dee trout 'just out of the water'. At the High Class Family Grocers, Mr and Mrs Humphreys assured me that my crumpled list of hieroglyphs would be somehow translated into reality and delivered up to Hafod on Thursday.

'The old van knows that track,' I was told. Apparently the ladies had been regular customers. Anxious to take advantage of this miraculous arrangement, I suggested that if, in future, Ellis Greengrocer could drop in an order of fish for me, it could be brought up with my groceries. The two shops were only a few doors apart.

'I'm sure Mr Ellis wouldn't mind, if you wouldn't,' I babbled on. 'I could ring him on a Thursday . . . '

Behind his spectacles, Mr Humphreys's face had clouded. His wife's expression was even more grim.

'I'm afraid that wouldn't be possible. Not with Mr Ellis.'

'Oh dear.' I was taken aback. I thought of the little old lady on the bus. I had obviously come across yet another deep-laid seam of antagonism lurking beneath the sociable Welsh surface.

'Question of property . . . Right of way . . . Been going on for years . . . '

Changing the subject to marmalade, I picked up a pot of Celtic Maid and decided it was time to move on to Myfanwy at the bakery.

'Fresh cobs have just come in this minute,' announced the grandmotherly lady in a pink pinafore. 'I hear you on the wireless,' she added slyly. 'So don't think we don't know you!'

'*Woman's Hour*,' agreed a fellow shopper. 'I always enjoy it, except for the bit with the lady doctor. Really embarrassing that is.'

'Got one of your books from the library last year!' This was the young lady bringing in the custard tarts. 'Pity about the ending though. Sad, wasn't it?'

The grandmother was consoling. 'Never mind. You'll be writing another one soon, I expect. So peaceful it'll be for you up at Hafod, away from that old London.'

Laden with far too much bread, I made my escape. Being

confronted with this other strange life of mine was like catching sight of myself in a distorting mirror. It was also a reminder that before too long, Welsh freedom would vanish and I'd have to be back to London for a while to make some more programmes.

As I stood on the pavement balancing my bags, I felt a hand on my arm.

'You're not going to carry all that off the bus, surely,' said a familiar voice. 'Will's brought the Land Rover down today so we can put our shopping in.'

Megan, in a neat straw hat, somehow looked out of place in town, which was how I was beginning to feel, and only too ready to go home. But, once rid of our shopping, she had another suggestion.

'What about a quick pop-in to Benny's? Benny the Bid,' she explained, seeing my blank look. 'Tuesday's sale-day and I usually look in to see if there's anything tempting.'

Temptation comes naturally to me where sales are concerned. Both my South Wales grandmother and my mother had been experts at sniffing out half-price treasure with well-concealed cracks and flaws, whether it was a country house affair in a marquee, or a weekly knock-down in some dusty storage rooms. Being Llangollen, Benny's sale had a style of its own. Half the town seemed to be there, some crowded into the huge iron shed at the back of the main street, the rest gathered outside in the yard where the sun was shining and the auctioneer, the famous Benjamin Jones, was holding court on his moveable rostrum.

I remembered Benny from my early visits to his Wrexham salerooms as a newly married woman, looking for bargains. Like all good auctioneers, he never forgot a face. I knew I'd been spotted, even tucked away with Megan at the back of the crowd.

'Glad to welcome newcomers to our little gathering,' he boomed. 'Especially a returned native, back from her travels round the world.'

There was a twinkle in my direction. Then with a brush of his red whiskers, it was time for the familiar impassioned plea as the tide of chatter rose again.

'But, ladies! Ladies, please! I must remind you, if you want to talk there are more suitable places for indulging.' He drew himself up to his full five feet. 'Meanwhile, we come to the grand finale of the day.'

The grand finale seemed to consist of the usual end-of-sale shipwreck, tables littered with pots and pans and crockery oddments, a stack of old picture frames, a couple of mattresses, and sundry items yet to be identified including a birdcage and some late lamented gentleman's clutch of walking sticks.

'The big stuff's gone, of course,' Megan whispered. This time the 'locusts' appeared to be a pack of wolfish-looking men in shirt-sleeves, smoking together in the doorway. 'Dealers from England.' She nodded darkly. 'Just one of them bids and then they split it all up between them. They go round the farms and cottages too. Persuade the old people to give them bits and pieces out of the barns for next to nothing, then get ridiculous prices for them in the antique shops in Shrewsbury. Worse than tinkers, they are.'

'Well, they won't catch me out!' said a voice behind us.

'Gwyneth!' exclaimed Megan. And then, 'Bethan!'

Against a counterpoint of bidding I was introduced to the two sisters, both confusingly like Megan, except that one was darker and the other plumper.

During the conversation Gwyneth slipped in a quick nod for an ironing board. Not noticing, Megan was flustered to find she was bidding against her, until Benny kindly rectified the misunderstanding in favour of Gwyneth.

'Concentrate now, ladies,' he admonished. 'A sale needs concentration!'

In front of us, one dedicated bargain-hunter was distributing Welshcakes.

'Sale famine!' she joked, offering us some. 'That's what you get by this time of the day!' The tempo had quickened as some extra items were brought out by the young porter, Medwyn, a promising nephew of Benny's who was being groomed for promotion, no doubt. A Victorian carpet was mentioned, 'worn in places, but still good for another few years'.

On the spur of the moment, thinking of Hafod's linoleum, I began to bid and, within minutes, found it knocked down to me for £22.

'I haven't actually seen it,' I confessed, handing up the money.

'You're standing on it, madam!' called Medwyn, to some amusement. 'And a proper bargain it is – good owners too.'

So it seemed. I turned back a torn corner of the dusty Oriental specimen to discover the edging neatly bound with a label in faded copperplate. Bending down, I read, 'Music Room Fire Damage 1894'.

'Comes from a gentry house in Cerrigydrudion,' someone next to me said. 'Just been turned into a nursing home.'

I looked up at the handsome woman with the mass of dark hair and suddenly saw Morfydd from Minera. Behind the disguise of middle age there she still was, the fourth-form prodigy in her Welsh hat and frilly apron bowing to the applause for her eisteddfod solo.

'Grove Park, 1945,' I said, suddenly back at the end of the front row, with a pain in my stomach at the thought of mounting the platform to read my third-prize poem on Valle Crucis. ' . . . O'er the old Abbey the wind softly blows . . . ' And so on.

'I heard you were coming back to Wales,' she said.

'You live here then?'

'Not far. My husband is a teacher and I work in the library at Ruthin, so we haven't exactly moved around.' She drew me aside. 'Talking of Grove Park though – you remember Winnie, our English mistress?'

'Who could forget her?'

She nodded towards a hamper of books I hadn't noticed

before. 'Those are hers. She died last month. Still on her own she was.' I moved to look more closely, but Morfydd stopped me with a nudge in the ribs.

'Don't show interest. You never know! See who's looking through them?'

A small antiquarian figure in long skirts was bent over the hamper, examining the contents with intense concentration. 'That's our local historian,' hissed Morfydd. 'The famous Miss Parry-Williams. But I think it's Dr Johnson's *Dictionary* she's after. So you've got a chance.'

There was the scent of conspiracy in the air, so dear to Welsh hearts. I wanted those books more dearly than I could have imagined. But the idea of confrontation made me nervous.

'Only some old books,' I told Megan. Already, though, Benny had caught onto the drama of the situation.

'The last item of the day,' he called. 'And a very important one. Books belonging to a highly respected member of the teaching profession, the late Miss Wynne-Jones, affectionately known to her pupils as Winnie.' His oratorial vibrato rose to fresh heights. 'And with us no doubt are some of those very pupils, who owe so much to Miss Wynne-Jones's dedication to literature.' A glance was flashed in my direction. 'Grove Park School,' he intoned, opening a sample book. 'And here inside is stamped their famous motto, Inter Silvas Quaerere Verum – To Seek Truth Among the Groves. A noble aim indeed!'

After this peroration the actual bidding was almost a relief. Right from the start Miss Parry-Williams and I were the sole combatants, her beady gaze interlocked with mine as we duelled together up the scale from £5 to £35. At this point Benny decided to spice up the contest by taking out the Johnson *Dictionary* to sell separately. Having acquired Winnie's hamper for a mere forty, I was more than content to let the revered historian take Dr Johnson, or at least half of him. The mighty calf-bound edition was in two volumes and for the sake of peace Benny announced a judgment along the lines of Solomon's baby.

'Hardly a scholarly solution,' snapped Miss Parry-Williams afterwards. 'But at least I have the A to K section.'

For a couple of tenners the Johnsonian definition of everything from L to Z (Zootomist. A diffecter of the bodies of brute beafts) was pretty good value, I thought. I hope Winnie would have agreed, though it was the sight-unseen hamper that was my real prize. There was no time for an examination of the contents. The next minute it was stacked in the back of the Land Rover with the rest of our sales trophies, including a three-legged stool acquired by Megan to compensate for the loss of the ironing board. Still tremulous after the excitement of battle, the two of us squeezed into the front next to Will.

'Sale fever!' teased Will, shaking his head. The rain predicted by the heron began to fall as we bumped up the track to Hafod. 'Lucky you didn't try to get all this onto the Why-Walk.' As we got out he gave me one of his endearing smiles. 'Anyway, you've got your magic carpet. You'll be able to fly from one end of Wales to the other on that!'

Ceremonially unrolled, it fitted into the parlour as if made for it, even though it was something of a come-down from the music room at Nant-y-Garth Hall. As for the books, I wanted to look through those on my own. So, when Will and Megan had gone, I stacked them out carefully on the dining-table, the well-worn volumes of poetry, the schoolroom editions of Shakespeare, Chaucer and Milton, the Victorian jumble of essays and biography. Unpacked, they exuded the mysterious scent of all old books, a compound of damp leather bindings and brittle paper much fingered. There was also a lingering sense of those invisible readers who had pored over the pages and somehow left behind something of themselves between the lines.

Being Winnie's books, her presence was so real I felt some temerity about even opening them. I looked for her name first of all, that spiky signature so familiar from homework essays and school reports. But something strange had happened. In every book the top right-hand corner of the flyleaf had either been torn away, or else the name itself erased with an angry scribble. It was as if she wanted to blot herself out from her own memory. I remembered rumours of nervous breakdowns even when we were at school. There was sometimes a wildness about that frizzled grey head of hair and the prophetically-rolling eyes as she read from 'The Ancient Mariner', one of her favourites. Perhaps at the end irrationality had taken over when she was alone and ill. Yet I remembered the letters she sent me whenever I had a book published, or a piece about me had appeared in one of the papers. Sometimes she wrote to congratulate. Sometimes she took me to task for falling below the expected standard. Either way, the letters touched me, as did the memory of them now as I sat with her books in my hands, and her voice in my ear, rapid, incisive, always heartfelt, even when most severe.

Turning the pages of various verse collections I saw she had treated the poets with the same passion for perfection she had bestowed on her pupils. Against Browning's 'Pippa Passes' she had written 'Excellent. First class expression of mood'. Tennyson's 'Lotus Eaters' received less favourable comments for its 'Overblown language. More restraint should have been observed'. Wordsworth himself suffered a terse 'Could do better than this' for his 'Lucy Gray', I noticed. These marginal markings were in her usual magenta ink. Perhaps they were a kind of shorthand for the lessons she was to deliver to us. Perhaps they were a compulsive return to her teaching role long after her retirement. At any rate they brought back Winnie in a way that nothing else could.

I was looking unconsciously for the Gerard Manley Hopkins she used to quote to us in her diatribe on the English poets' debt to Wales and Welsh literature. And there it was, that magical passage of his from *In the Valley of the Elwy*.

Lovely the woods, waters, meadows, combes, vales,
All the air things wear that build this world of Wales . . .
Against this was scribbled another Hopkins line
And sheep-flock clouds like worlds of wool

(from Penmaen Pool)

'V.G.' was marked against this extract.

On the endpaper, a few pages on, were some notes under the heading *The English Literary Invasion*. Back on her favourite theme, she made a list of visiting writers and poets whose excursions into North Wales had provided them with the secret inspiration for their best work – according to Winnie at least. At the top, heavily underlined was Shelley ('Lived at Tremadoc while writing 'Queen Mab' – foolish youth pretended to be shot at in order to run away from debt!') Next came the maligned Wordsworth ('See "The Prelude" on climbing Snowdon, a much better effort than his effusion on a Welsh harper in "The Excursion"). Thomas Love Peacock was also on the roll-call. ('Actually married a Welsh girl after keeping her waiting for eight years') as was Lord Tennyson, 'on the trail of the Arthurian legend at Llyn Beris'. (See also 'The Lady of Shalott'!)

Appended to these were some other jottings – Hazlitt in the Vale of Llangollen, De Quincey hitchhiking through the Denbighshire wilds ('A feckless teenager as in *Confessions of an English Opium-Eater*'). Even Dr Johnson was included ('Puffing and panting up alongside his beloved Mrs Thrale, that excellent Welsh woman'). Finally the admired Coleridge had been scribbled in on a walking tour with knapsack and a five-foot stave (carved with an eagle's head, Winnie noted). Why was the unlikely name of Wrexham added here, I wondered? Then I remembered it was where the youthful poet had caught an unexpected glimpse of his former sweetheart, Mary Evans, and retreated in confusion to Ruthin, sixteen miles away. 'Coward!' Winnie had exploded in brackets.

Underneath the list Winnie had written. 'N.B. Form VI A

to examine these links in their work for Higher School Certificate (Literature Section).'

Was I one of that particular year, I wondered? Alas, I have no recollection at all of these suggested studies. But, better late than never, Winnie had now whetted my appetite. The idea of catching up with these literary lions along our own lanes and valleys was a beguiling one, so was the notion of sharing their experiences of Wales and the Welsh. Once again Winnie had provided inspiration and set the agenda though it would be some time before I could follow it up. Hafod would exert an ever-increasing pull on me, especially with R and the family here.

That night I went to bed with Coleridge. I was curious to know what he had been writing in 1794, the year of his tour. I found the answer in a poem called 'Pantisocracy', the name of the ideal republican community he dreamed of so passionately at that time. Some lines in the middle seemed to chime in with my Wales anyway, or was it just the effect of the full moon streaming through the uncurtained window? 'I seek the cottaged dell,' he wrote,

Where Virtue calm with careless step may stray,
And dancing to the moonlight roundelay
The wizard Passions weave an holy spell.

Falling asleep, I wondered if the wizard Passions were dancing in the moonlight for Will and Megan and for old Mrs Roberts up on the haunted fields of Pant Glas farm . . .

8

ALARMS AND
EXCURSIONS

'Pen-y-Bryn here.' On the telephone Will's voice was strangely formal, echoing along the overhead line that stretched between us for all of two hundred yards. 'It's about the post.'

'Oh dear,' I said. There had been a problem recently about some repairs to the corner of the sheep fence at the top of the bank. 'Come down again, has it?'

There was a pause for thought, then a chuckle.

'No, no! Not that kind of post. I mean the what-do-y'call – the mail. Dewi says he's sorry he couldn't get up to Hafod this morning because we're dipping.'

'Sorry?' The line was developing its usual crackle.

'Sheep-dipping. We had to block the lane to get them across to the brook. So he's left your delivery here at the farm.'

'That's all right. Nothing special, is there?'

'Just the one letter, it is. For your husband. From London,' he went on.

I broke in. 'Don't worry. He'll pick it up when he comes for the milk.'

The last thing R needed was a reminder of work. He'd only just arrived for the late summer legal vacation and was already absorbed in the demands and distractions of this new life in Wales. At this moment he was on his knees investigating a fall of soot in the parlour chimney, heralded by the discovery of a dead jackdaw.

'If we're out he's sure to see it,' Will told me. 'I've left it safe under the stone on top of the milk-churn.'

As it happened the churn had, for some reason, been moved next to the railings where the pigs were enclosed. It only took a nudge from one inquisitive snout for the missive to be dislodged for closer inspection. It hadn't actually been opened and read but it was evident that the large embossed envelope had been rooted over in the process, which was how the imposing document from HM appointing R a Metropolitan Stipendiary Magistrate had acquired its distinctive patina of mud and manure. The scarlet seal remained intact and, as R said, sniffing it, it actually smelled quite clean, almost antiseptic in fact.

'That'll be the sheep-dip,' I told him.

R nodded thoughtfully. Apparently the letter's final resting-place was the adjoining sheep-pen, blown there by the odd puff of wind perhaps, unless the tidy-minded pigs used it as their rubbish bin.

We toasted the news in Sammy Sparks's sloe gin. He'd kindly brought us a sample bottle along with his delivery of the second-hand fridge and the third-hand cooker. Although it was exciting to be appointed to the London Bench with a court of his own at Tower Bridge, the reality of it was hard to envisage. Hafod and the here-and-now wiped out everything else. As both of us agreed, the saga of the letter was just another example of the maverick spirit of the place which liked to remind us that nothing was sacred. Marooned in our mountain fastness, it was a miracle that anything behaved normally, ourselves included.

Hence there was the tendency of water in the taps to run backwards, for smoke from the fires to blow into the rooms at the same time as rising up through the chimneys. Slugs refused to stay out in the garden but inched their way beneath doors and windows to make themselves at home with humans, bringing the bindweed with them. Spiders toiled up every plughole to festoon bath and sink with elaborate webs.

The weather was just as disobedient. If the barometer pointed to a fine spell, a Wagnerian storm-cloud would descend. If rain was predicted, sure enough the valley would turn out its own pocketful of sunshine, complete with the double rainbow that was a local speciality. Human communications fell under the same spell of misrule. Why else, if the phone rang, was it so often a crossed line that refused to be uncrossed, delivering urgent messages for ghostly recipients in another part of the Principality altogether? Even the clocks refused to conform, slyly gathering speed or stopping altogether. As a result, the hours of the day led a dance of their own, sometimes dissolving into thin air in a way we called Hafod Timemelt.

By now R and I were well adjusted to this state of affairs. More than once we reminded ourselves that it was only natural for paradise to have rules of its own. And, from this viewpoint, paradise was no cliché, though Eden seemed a better word as the sun rose, glinting through the rowan trees on a still summer morning. A precarious innocence hung over the mountain then, the air of a first morning ever. A line from Blake would catch it even as it flew. 'Piping down the valleys wild' was the mantra that always ran through my head at that moment, even though I could never remember exactly where it belonged.

Fortunately the cheerful anarchy of everyday life kept our feet on the ground. For Howard and Vanessa, arriving for the last weeks of student holidays, it all seemed curiously familiar, a kind of reincarnation of holidays spent in the wilds of Arabia and the remote South Sea islands. For both of them, the stolid regime of boarding school had always cut short those storybook adventures. Now, in Wales, we all had a chance to reinvent ourselves, to celebrate freedom in another place that was off the map and out of bounds, yet undeniably a place where we belonged. This was the most important thing of all, for them as it was for me.

Between them, they took over the 'wing' which had been home to Ned the quarryman's family, filling the rooms with the flotsam and jetsam of the early 70s. Howard, a dark and intense young man moving on from art college to the University of East Anglia, set himself up with his guitar and his *Private Eye* posters, his paints and canvases, scribbled poems and unfinished novels of sub-Waugh satire. Vanessa, five years younger, was the actress-to-be, blonde and bubbly, thrilled to have been recruited into the National Youth Theatre with Central Drama School on the horizon. Lists were already being run up for next year's birthday parties. An old piano was also installed, which promptly fell through the floor of the so-called study, bringing Mr Jenkins to the rescue with tape-measure and new boards.

What about the past, though? Who had lived here in the old days, they wanted to know. Vanessa was already improvising on the ghost she claimed to have seen on the stairs, a tiny white-haired lady in a grey shawl. Howard was investigating on a more scholarly level and brought home a scrap of paper from the Ruthin Archives which took us back to 1881, the year of the census.

Together we pored over the names recorded as the inhabitants of Numbers 1, 2 and 3, Hafod-y-Fron (Hafod on the Mountain). David Pugh, aged 28, labourer, from Merioneth, emerged from the shadows as head of his household, with his 34-year-old wife, Ellen, and their two children, Mary and Robert, both described touchingly as 'scholars' even though the little boy was only four. Next door was a Thomas Rogers, another labourer, married to one Jane (38), whose fifteen-year-old daughter Mary Griffiths was obviously the offspring of an earlier liaison. Finally came Jane Jones who, at 68, was also designated head of a household, even though she was a widow, and no doubt ruled the little row of cottages with a rod of iron.

'Two Joneses and two Marys,' said Vanessa, already deep into the different characters. 'That must have led to problems.'

'Especially sharing the wash-house at the end,' said Howard, who had seen an old plan of the site. 'At least each house had its own privy.'

Not with an owl in it, I thought. That was later . . .

So we now had the sense of an earlier set of inhabitants, going back beyond Mrs Roberts's memories. It brought home to me the sad gap in my own family tree. Both my father and mother died just before we found Hafod. At least there was my bachelor brother, Renfrey, the reluctant accountant, trundling up from Wrexham in his decrepit Volvo for Sunday lunch, entertaining us with his collection of vintage jazz records and his stories of other Ellis eccentrics. R's mother was brought up for her 90th birthday, pleased to see her grandfather's presentation inkstand on the desk. As chairman of the reception committee for Queen Victoria's visit to the nearby village of Ruabon, he had the nerve-racking task of escorting the two princesses down the mine without encountering a speck of coal-dust.

'So he deserved his inkstand, didn't he?' as my mother-in-law put it.

She herself, gentle soul, was somewhat alarmed at finding us 'so far off the beaten track'. But her younger sister, Elsie, concentrated bravely on the view, declaring it to be 'Handsome! Really handsome!' We all wondered what R's formidable father would have made of Hafod if he had lived to see it. Perhaps it was just as well he would never be confronted with a place that defied every rule in his iron regime of domestic law and order.

Meanwhile Howard was eager for us to look further afield. He'd already explored the potential of our own half-acre by drawing up an eighteenth-century-style design whereby the impenetrable tanglewood at the top of the bank would be miraculously transformed into something called The Cathedral Walk. Now he'd acquired a large-scale map of our valley and the surrounding mountains. On this he drew a large circle with Hafod at the centre, circles being the essential element of all good Celtic mythology and most prehistoric remains as well. Did we realize, he asked us, that, within this three-mile radius, there were at least half a dozen famous landmarks dating from the Bronze Age to medieval days? Here we were right at the heart of a sort of magic time-capsule, so shouldn't we get out and have a look at some of these relics? What had we been doing since we'd arrived at the house?

'Getting it ready to live in,' was my reply.

'And sorting out one or two water problems,' added R.

It was a reminder that the first relic to be inspected was our well. The word itself was a highly emotive one, conjuring up a rich variety of picturesque images. Even as we set out on the walk there, a sunburnt half-mile along the mountainside, Vanessa was agog with stories of legendary local wells she'd found in a dog-eared guidebook left behind by the Misses Sinclair.

'Just imagine!' she chattered, bouncing ahead of us through the waist-high bracken followed by new labrador, Rosie. 'Up on the moors at Llandegla there's one that actually works miracles. People used to come from all over Wales to be cured of epilepsy just by drinking the water – oh, and they had to walk round it three times carrying a live chicken.'

'What happened then?' we asked.

'You put the chicken's beak into your mouth and your fits would be transferred to the bird.'

'How would you know?'

'Because it staggered away and fell down dead.'

'Not surprisingly,' said someone.

But Vanessa was breathlessly embarked on another Grand Guignol scene. 'What about St Dyfnog's well at Llanrhaeadr? He did penance by standing for *years* under a waterfall in a hair shirt and an iron chain, and ever after the water could cure scabs and smallpox and the itch, and even deafness and dumbness.'

Eighteen-year-old Aled, a sturdy-looking nephew of Will's who was our guide, pricked up his ears.

'What Llanrhaeadr was that, Vanessa?'

'Llanrhaeadr-yng-Nghinmeirch.' She reeled off the syllables with relish. Not for nothing had she spent eight years at a famous Welsh girls' school at Dolgellau.

'The Church of the Waterfall at Cinmeirch,' translated Aled, looking impressed by her accent.

'But Vanessa,' her brother expostulated. 'Those were holy wells, not domestic ones.'

'All wells are holy in Wales,' declared Aled who, for some reason, was carrying a small stepladder over his shoulder. 'A spring comes free from God, my grandfather used to say. In the old days you didn't build a cottage unless there was a well nearby.'

Nobody mentioned that this one wasn't exactly nearby from Hafod's point of view. There was still no sign of it as the winding sheep-track came to an end at a fence. The ladder was now explained as Aled slung it over the rusty barbed wire. If we had gone along by the bottom lane there would be no such obstacles, he reminded us. But this was the shortest way and at least there was less climbing involved.

The fence manoeuvred, we found ourselves under a canopy of ancient oak trees that looked holy indeed, sacred perhaps if you conjured up pictures of the druidical rites associated with such groves. Through the leaves, we could see like a dream in the distance the ruined abbey of Valle Crucis. Up here the two sites seemed linked somehow. Perhaps the unearthly beauty of the valley had always made it a place of worship, the pagan gods preparing the way for the white-robed Cistercians with their own secret ceremonies of prayer and supplication.

Now, as then, the yellow gorse blazed over every slope like a hundred burning bushes. Faintly we could hear the trickle of water coming from under ground and growing louder. Then, all at once, there was the well. Or rather there was a battered black tank wedged into the hillside with a few old bricks. On top was the sheet of corrugated iron mentioned by Will, firmly anchored down with a large stone. It was a singularly prosaic object with no sign of a sylvan fountain or even a waterfall. The pipe that fed it, like the one that led away from it, was buried deep in the turf and yet there was a magic about the secret flow of water coming apparently from nowhere, always renewing itself from some underground spring high above us. When Howard and Aled raised the lid, I dipped in a cup from our picnic bag and we passed around a ritual libation. It was crystal clear, yet tasting mysteriously of the mountain, fresh but ancient and incredibly cold, like stone on the tongue. I thought of it snaking its subterranean way down to the farm pumps and the cottages of fifty years ago when the pipes were laid.

'Before that they'd come here with buckets, I suppose,' Aled said. 'Or perhaps there might have been a smaller spring a bit closer, perhaps by the old barn there.'

We looked down at the worn slates of a derelict building in the field below us. We were scrambling down the hill towards it now, on our way back to Hafod by the bottom lane. But Aled seemed anxious for us to avoid it.

'Not a good place,' he said, in a low voice.

'You're not repairing it, then?' I asked.

He shook his head, his expression was closed.

'Best to let it go. A bad thing happened there once, a long time ago.'

Through the trees we could see the glint of the little river winding its way along the bottom of the valley. It was very hot and when Aled said there was a pool under the bridge deep enough for diving, Howard and Vanessa disappeared with him across the fields.

But, like R, I was drawn to the barn. Close up, you could see that one section of it had already collapsed. The wooden supports had given way and the upturned iron roof had settled deep into the overgrown hazel and hawthorn, as if the Ark had finally foundered on the mountainside after the Flood. But the main barn miraculously kept its gabled shape, held together by the old stones that were no doubt taken from the abbey ruins as farmers did in other centuries. The holes in the slates were patched with purple willow-herb though the beams beneath still held firm. At the front, the two halves of the stable door leaned forward on gaping hinges, bleached like driftwood.

Something made me reach into a chink in the wall. Tucked away at the back was an ancient glove, the leather roughly stitched and hardened by time into the shape of the unknown hand which had left it there at the end of a day's work.

Something else made me put it back again. By the same instinct, we felt unwilling to go inside. Instead we stood on the threshold, catching sight of fragments of another life, a broken pitchfork, a horse's chain hanging from its nail, cattle-stalls deep in nettles. In the shadows you could make out the enclosure where the hired labourers must have slept and fed in the old days, with the hayloft above. There was a blackened square on the wall where fires had been lit, empty window-frames that no longer held the familiar valley views, only green leaves thrusting through from the ash trees that had rooted in the rubble. A few swallows circled in and out again from under the eaves. Otherwise there was the silence and stillness of a long-deserted place. Yet somehow it was not empty. The air held a presence that was almost tangible, a sense of resignation, even despair.

So something had happened here, strong enough to print itself on the future. Perhaps Megan will tell me about it some time, I thought, and I was right. It was a winter afternoon, months later, and we had been out looking for the old drovers' track over the mountain. At one point our way took us directly past the barn. Huddled below us in the grey light, it seemed to have lost a few more stones, the slate roof dipping just a little further over the doorway.

'It was Will's great-grandfather,' Megan said quietly, as if I had asked her a question. 'He hanged himself in there, poor man. Money worries and the loneliness, you know. There's more than one of the old hill-farmers took that way out when things got bad. Still do,' she added, half to herself. 'In Wales, anyway.' She glanced at me with a trace of a smile. 'They say we Welsh have a melancholy streak, don't they?'

We walked on for a bit.

'He was living on his own?' I asked.

She nodded. 'But he loved his dogs. Sent them away down to his brother's farm that evening, when' – she stopped. 'When it was time,' she said, after a moment. She put her hand on my arm, 'Will's family don't talk about it. It's supposed to be bad luck. So it's left in the past.' She looked over her shoulder. 'Like the old barn.'

Behind us, our own dogs still hung back where a broken gate-post marked the way down.

'They never like coming past just there.'

No more was said. Dusk was falling and we turned for home.

9

Relics and Revelations

There is always a strange time on the mountain when autumn and winter seem interchangeable. One day all was brilliance, a low afternoon sun fanning the forests to flame, the slopes of dead bracken gleaming amber and bronze beneath the smoky blue of the heather moors. In this kind of light even our wilderness garden could be viewed through rose-coloured glasses. Scarlet tatters lit up the ruins of the willow-herb. In the hawthorn tree, a bullfinch and a robin flashed their different reds among the ruby-coloured berries like a cheap birthday card. This was still autumn when the steps are warm to sit on and there are the buzzards to watch, always three of them, floating to dizzy heights on the soft currents of air. On the stone next to me a lone bumble-bee disentangled himself from a spider's web, stumbling away to live another day.

The next morning we found ourselves in a different country. A killing frost had come down in the night, stealthily, like a wicked spell. Outside, each branch and leaf was encrusted in white. The sun had gone out, seemingly forever. In its place, a misty chill shrouded everything in a grey half-light. This new stillness was so complete it was as if the earth's circulation had suddenly stopped. Crystallized roses and waxen berries had the air of funeral memorials, so did the yellow leaves plastered beneath the glassy hollows on the path.

Walking down the lane for the milk it was reassuring to see my breath in front of me. From behind came the sound of furtive footfalls. But it was only leaves again, dropping frozen onto iron ruts, one at a time. When the gales came, they would be shed in a rush. That might even be tomorrow, with day after day of bitter wind and rain, so that you felt such weather would never end, until the following week when autumn might be back again. Then people would say that winter was still only a flash in the pan – *dros dro*, for the time being. The best days were those which started with an overlap of the two seasons. First thing, the fields might be white with frost. Slowly, as the sun rose higher over the mountain, the valley would become half silver and half gold until the light spread to the shadow side of the valley, driving the frost before it like an incoming tide.

Summer itself had been and gone. But for me its essence was trapped in the six shining jars of bramble jelly ranged like trophies on one of Mr Jenkins's shelves. The raw materials were humble enough – a heap of Hafod blackberries torn with bleeding fingers from a forest of brambles, together with some windfalls from Pen-y-Bryn's apple-trees, and a large bag of damp sugar. The scent of it was richly potent as it simmered in the brass pan that had belonged to my South Wales grandmother. Fortunately I had her instructions to guide me, a torn page of spidery writing from her recipe book, dashed off no doubt in between her excitable (and one-sided) conversations with my grandfather, Fred, deep in his *Western Mail*.

'Drop a spoonful onto a saucer and test with finger-tip,' was the mystical clue to the correct jelly moment. I did my best, having first let the juices drip all night through a strange flannel bag loaned by Megan.

'Better than the way old Mr Rogers used to make marmalade,' Will had said. He was referring to an eccentric Englishman who had retired many years ago to a tumbledown cottage higher up the valley. The oranges were brought up in a sack on the back of his donkey. The actual marmalade-making was simplicity itself, it seemed. 'I always strain it well,' Mr Rogers would croak cheerfully, adding, as he handed over a jar at Christmas time, 'Any old sock will do.'

Despite my misgivings, my jelly was a success, unlike the elderberry port. The cascades of luscious jet beads that hung from every elder tree had been too tempting to resist. Besides, the formula sounded simple enough, according to the WI cookery book given to me by Gwen, who was now a weekly visitor. She assured me that the port was reckoned to be one of the Institute's most successful inventions. So it seemed, at first. In fact, our rector's wife from Llandrillo sampled it with enthusiasm. It reminded her of something, she said, pondering a moment. Ah yes, Communion wine. That was it. What could be better, we asked ourselves.

Perhaps the explosion was some kind of reprimand for minor blasphemy. At any rate, what was meant to be a fine after-dinner liqueur discharged itself under the stairs in a deep purple spray that remained part of the decorative scheme for months.

Secondary fermentation was the official verdict. No doubt, as amateurs, we should have handed the process over to Gwen. But at the time my mind was focused not on elderberries but on the long-promised revelations about her true identity. These were related to me over several pots of tea as we sat face to face at the kitchen table one morning. The story was simple but extraordinary, with strong overtones of a Catherine Cookson novel. It told me as much about Welsh rural life of the time as it did about Gwen herself.

Back in the working-class Midlands of the 1950s a young woman from a broken home decided to escape from her grinding factory job to find a better way of life. Searching the newspapers, she answered an advertisement for a live-in domestic help. Within weeks she was ensconced under the roof of the kindly Mrs S-P and her husband, the Major, in the remote countryside of Denbighshire, surrounded by the rolling hills of the Dee valley and a few scattered farms.

'I'd never even seen a cow before,' was Gwen's way of putting it, sharp eyes sparkling at the absurdity of it all. In the village, a couple of miles away, the only language to be heard was Welsh. 'And they couldn't understand me either, because my English had such a funny accent. Talk about a language barrier!'

But as lady of the manor, Mrs S-P soon took things in hand. Gwen was given a ticket to the local Noson Lawen, a Welsh musical evening where she met a young man called Gwilym who worked for the Forestry. He was too shy to introduce himself to this good-looking girl from nowhere, he just gave the name of the farm where he lived with relations. But he found out her next day off and turned up at the back door, cap in hand, to ask if she was ready.

'Ready for what?' Gwen asked.

'A walk maybe,' came the answer in hesitant English.

So an evening stroll round the village became a regular feature of this unlikely friendship, with the tongue-tied Gwilym, wheeling his motorbike alongside her, while the locals voiced their opinions in Welsh. On one occasion, Gwen caught a word she knew, which was wife.

'So I jumped to the conclusion that he was married and I was cross he'd never told me. He was quite indignant. No, he wasn't, he said, but he'd like to be, if I'd have him.'

And so it turned out, with Mrs S-P and the Major providing the wedding reception. Gwilym's family were less enthusiastic. A prolonged silence greeted the bride-to-be on her first visit to the farm until an aged uncle came up with a vital question. 'You're a foreigner, then?'

But Gwen stood her ground. 'No, I'm British like you,' was her response, which didn't seem to cut much ice.

Attitudes were to change, though. Little did anyone know that within the next few years she would be baling hay, milking cows, docking sheep's tails and cornering temperamental bulls as if she'd been doing it all her life. The farm Gwilym took on was an ancient rambling place high up on the Eglwyseg rocks, ' . . . nettles up to the windows and rats running everywhere when we first moved in. The wagon had to be unloaded fast because the driver was due to pick up cattle for market in it.'

First the house itself had to be made habitable. The boiler had been used for pig-swill so that had to be cleaned out. 'But the first thing I did was to whitewash over the black patch on the wall where the old farmer had sat back after work every day of his life, finally passing away there.' Soon there were small children to be walked three miles to school into the next valley, shopping for food to be done via the Why-Walk bus another three miles away, water to be fetched from the brook when the plumbing broke down in the freezing Eglwyseg winters.

'I was on my mettle, I suppose,' was Gwen's only comment on this relentless survival course. 'My grandfather was a blacksmith, so perhaps that's where I get my practical streak. And I always remember him telling me that there was nothing in life you couldn't do, if you put your mind to it.'

Taking this motto to heart, Gwen rapidly produced order out of chaos and recreated herself in the process. Over the years, the spirited newcomer became a pillar of the rural community, leading light of the WI, the village fête and the local dog show as well as the most capable of hill-farming wives. Now in addition there was a weekly assignation to help keep Hafod in working order and to bring me up to date with a round-up of local news. This was a long-running scenario spiced with Midlands humour and Welsh drama which always made for compulsive listening.

'More of that another time,' was the usual signal for the end of the tea-break as dusters, Brasso and 'spider mop' were brought out, Gwen's favourite instruments in Hafod's transformation. With winter upon us, the laying and lighting of fires was an art of hers I took trouble to learn, especially the virtue of stoking up with one huge log overnight.

'It's what the Welsh say about love-affairs, isn't it?' she told me. 'Easier to kindle on a warm hearth than a cold one. Or some such nonsense,' she added briskly.

Oddly enough, winter proved to be the time best suited for exploration, the chance to get to know some of the historic sites listed on Howard's circular tour. The hump-backed files of hikers had vanished from the mountainside. The little lane that took you the back way over a stream to the loveliest of all those landmarks, Valle Crucis Abbey, was invitingly deserted under the bare trees. Being so close, less than half a mile away, I tended to think of the place not so much as a famous ruin as a next-door neighbour fallen on hard times, someone you could drop in on without ceremony. After all, this half-forgotten way winds along just under our sheep wall. Many a horseback procession of the good and the great must have jingled along it, passing the crumbling hovel that was the Hafod of those days without so much as a glance, as they made their way to the most prestigious holy building in Wales. That was in its fifteenth-century heyday when the genial Abbot Dafydd ab Ieuan held court there like a prince. 'A vigorous oak', 'a large-hearted falcon' were two of the images used to describe him. Another resident bard glowingly wrote of 'the flow of wine at his table and the gifts of gold . . . It's a life that is next to being in Heaven.' I walk the tracks of those processions almost every day, down the leafy tunnel where the lane narrows round between the hillside and the forest.

I wonder how the poets would have responded to a twentieth-century vision of the abbey, with a permanent settlement of caravans occupying the old monastic grounds. It was not that Victorian scenes were exactly secluded. According to an account of the 1870s I came across, sightseers brought over the border by the thrilling new railway had poured through the abbey at the rate of three thousand a year. The custodian of the day, a Miss Lloyd, had jotted down in her diary 'more cheap trips', adding irascibly, 'Scamps got over the fence again!' One memorable August Bank Holiday, a policeman had to be summoned to control the unruly crowds in the very heart of the hallowed ruins.

But now it was November, a hundred years later. The day was misty, turning to rain, and the place so silent I could watch a kestrel flickering in and out of the chancel archway in search of monastic mice. What had been one of the architectural wonders of the age, rising out of the Eglwyseg wilderness like a mirage, still clung to past glories – the rose carving on the great Gothic façade, the ribbed vaulting and delicate traceried windows. The days of wine and merrymaking seemed as unreal as a Hollywood musical, though. Somehow, with the building reduced to its bare essentials, it was easier to feel close to the thirteenth-century founders with their sheep and their fish ponds and their spartan rituals of eight daily services, starting with the cold and the dark of the two o'clock bell. In the quiet I could walk among the dead with reverence, touching the ancient stones that summoned up legendary names of bards and nobles, the Iolos and the Glyns and the abbey's founder, Madog ap Gruffudd, who was an ancestor of Owain Glyndŵr, the greatest prince of all.

It was no use looking for Glyndŵr's grave at the abbey. No one knows how he met his end, let alone where he is buried. I could remember my disappointment as a child passing the place known famously as Owain Glyndŵr's Mount, only to be told that it certainly contained no body. 'It's all that's left of his house,' I was told by my father. 'After the English soldiers destroyed it.'

It seemed to me a pretty feeble reminder of the brave hero of the history stories told us at school.

Nowadays I felt the same sense of anti-climax when I

found myself in the next valley, passing it again. The little hillock covered with trees is set back from the road on private land. To the passing motorist it would be barely noticeable apart from a giant sign directing one to a nearby snack bar, further along the road. In the circumstances it was difficult to imagine that on this spot Owain was formally proclaimed Prince of Wales, on September 16th 1400, before he rallied his troops for the last great rising against English rule.

'We nearly won, too,' Knowledge Edwards reminded me a few days later. In the way of the Welsh, he might have been talking about the local darts team. It was only six hundred years ago, after all, perhaps the best-remembered moment in Welsh history. 'Besides, Glyndŵr was a local man, remember – the family owned land in every valley.'

Since that first encounter on the Why-Walk bus I had been bumping into Knowledge from time to time in the town library. On this occasion his hoary head was bent over a large volume entitled *Great Welshmen of History*. What did it say about Glyndŵr's death, I asked him.

'Nothing for certain,' he said, taking off his glasses, his beady eyes watering with concentration. He passed the book over to Siân at the counter, with the directions to put it on my ticket because I would find it of interest.

'One theory is that he ended his days at his daughter's house in Herefordshire,' he went on. 'She'd married some lordly rogue who was after the Glyndŵr estates, they say. But at least she didn't die of starvation in the Tower of London like her sisters, and her mother too.'

By now we were next door at Ellis Greengrocers where Knowledge was absently turning over a few tomatoes to add to his book-bag. I was studying the cauliflowers with difficulty while following my companion's line of thought.

'You know the old belief, I expect? That the great man is only sleeping, awaiting the call to arms once again when his country most needs him. Remember King Arthur? Lying with his warriors in some secret cave in the mountainside until the spell is broken.' He shook his head. 'If only.'

Little Mrs Ellis, weighing out potatoes, looked up with interest.

'Excuse me, Mr Edwards. You're the expert now. Is it true that one of Arthur's knights was called Cai?'

Knowledge looked stumped, but only briefly. 'I believe you're right, Mrs Ellis.' Mrs Ellis looked pleased.

Apparently her grandson, now aged two, had been christened Cai the year before. His patriotic parents thought it was time for the name to be revived. And now, if you please, there were no less than five other Cai babies being wheeled around Llangollen.

As we left, he tapped the *Great Welshmen*, wedged on top of my shopping. 'Madog ap Gruffudd to David Lloyd George, not a bad bunch. And somewhere there, you'll find mention of the great Eliseg, King of Powys, long before Glyndŵr's days. There's no problem about where he's buried. Just a few hundred yards from your doorstep.' He winked at me sideways as he toddled away. 'Just look for the Pillar, that's all. Anyone will show you Eliseg's Pillar.'

I remembered that it was one of the sites marked up on our map, not more than a walk away across the fields. From a distance it looked much like any other stone pillar, not very tall and worn around the top. At hay-cutting time I would watch from the house as Will encircled it in his tractor, careful not to encroach on the great man's resting-place. It seemed to me an insignificant monument for a king, standing solitary on a rough pedestal in the middle of nowhere.

But Mr Edwards's book soon corrected this idea. Far from being insignificant, it was a remarkable monument, unique, in fact. Old Eliseg – one of my own Ellis tribe, I liked to think – had been buried here well over a thousand years ago. This made the pillar itself, raised by his great grandson, Concenn, in the early 800s, the oldest inscribed cross in Britain.

For a cross was what it had once been. But this idolatrous

symbol was torn down by the barbarians of the Civil War. By one of those rare strokes of luck, however, the Welsh antiquarian, Edward Lhuyd, took the trouble to write down and translate the words of the inscription left on the broken shaft. That was in 1696. Now, here was I, standing in front of it, able to read these words in my own hand. I had scribbled them out from the book on the back of an envelope before setting out, giving thanks to the great Dr Lhuyd for this minor miracle. On the stone itself a series of blurred markings was all that could be made out now of the thirty-one lines of Latin miniscules.

They were carved and signed by a scribe named Commarch, 'who made this writing at the request of King Concenn'. It was endearing, I thought, that the writer made sure his name would be remembered in history. But it was the great Eliseg who was commemorated here, a founding hero of this country, 'he who recovered the land of Powys from the English with fire and sword'.

I looked at the battleground around me, patrolled by munching sheep. The forests above could still hide an army of Welsh guerillas before they came rampaging down on the camps of the invaders. A wintry sun was slipping behind the rim of the Berwyns. Soon the light would be gone. For a moment a final gleam slanted across the pillar throwing the markings into relief. I wanted to touch the surface, imagining it to feel like a message in braille, but the iron railings lay between us.

As the shadows came down, I thought about the remains beneath. Had he met his end in the fighting, bloodied and disfigured by the fire and the sword, before victory was won, or had he lived on to a revered old age, one of the last links with the legendary days of Roman rule? He was, after all, a direct descendant of the emperor, Magnus Maximus, or so claimed our industrious scribe.

It was much later that I came across the story that was to fix Eliseg in my mind more clearly than any litany of dates and genealogies. It was tucked away in one of those early Victorian guide-books to celebrated beauty spots. The author was a historian called W T Simpson, a local man with an inquisitive mind. In his researches he managed to track down an aged labourer who had been employed in resetting the pillar in 1779. Almost fifty years had gone by but it was a moment not easily forgotten. It seemed that when the tumulus was opened, the remains of a very tall man were revealed, still painted with the gold of a sacred burial. With some awe, the workmen reinterred what was left of the king, wrapping and sealing him up in his grassy pyramid like some Welsh pharaoh of old. Then Mr Simpson asked an ordinary enough question, 'Were the bones well preserved?'

The old man paused for a moment. 'They broke like gingerbread,' he said.

10

THE LAST SQUIRE
OF ERDDIG

Surrounded by so many historic landmarks, there was no escaping the past, not even my own. Memories of school excursions and family outings were coloured by such places. One above all was to stake a new claim in my life as time went by. This was Erddig, some ten miles along the road from Llangollen to Wrexham.

Even as a child my imagination was coloured by this mysterious house. The Wynns of Wynnstay, the Myddeltons of Chirk Castle and the wily Lord Trevor might represent the powerful aristocracy in our part of the Principality, but they were remote figures who did not impinge upon our everyday world in any way. As far as I was concerned the Yorkes of Erddig held a far greater fascination.

For a start, the owner of Erddig was simply known as the Squire which seemed to me a more romantic form of address than any of the usual titles. The Hall, as it was called, was quite close to the outskirts of Wrexham town. It was our own stately home, standing in our own kind of landscape, which was a surreal mixture of colliery slag-heaps and rolling heather-covered moors. We never set eyes on the actual house. It was a private place, hidden in woods and for children this was an essential part of Erddig's magic. The lodge at the gates was deserted and derelict, but the park beyond was a paradise, open to all. Sprawling up hill and down dale, it was like no other park I knew, wonderfully wild, its paths thick with beech leaves in the autumn and bluebells in the spring. Every summer when I was small I had my birthday picnic there. The slopes were for three-legged races and the river at the bottom was for paddling. But, over the bridge, where the drive led up to the Hall, was forbidden territory even on Standard IV nature walks led by our headmaster, Mr Davies.

In the park we always looked out for the Squire of that time whose name was Simon Yorke. But we never saw him. My father told me he was a recluse. Someone who shut himself up in his house and spoke to nobody, he explained. On Sunday mornings, though, there was often a brief glimpse of him at the parish church, sitting at the front in the family pew. He was a stiff, remote-looking man who reminded me of pictures of the new king, George VI, except that the king was sometimes smiling, if he was with Lilibet and Margaret Rose and the corgis. Simon had no children and no wife either and was never seen to smile. He came to church with his mother, a frail old lady in black, and they made their departure in silence, driving away in a rundown-looking black car.

Many were the tales told of the Squire's peculiar ways, especially after old Mrs Yorke died and he was in the Hall alone apart from a housekeeper. He lived by candlelight, it seemed, surrounded by fierce dogs. No callers were allowed. Even the postman had to leave the letters in the main lodge. He still went hunting, though, they said. But when the meet was held at Erddig any ladies who needed to visit the lavatory were directed to the bushes. There was no problem here, someone added, because the gardens had become a total wilderness.

As a small girl addicted to reading, I sometimes pictured myself encountering the lonely Squire in the park one day, by accident, perhaps when he was out on horseback. If I greeted him politely enough, he might prove not to be such an ogre after all. He might return the greeting, the ice would be broken and a friendship struck up. Invitations to explore the house with my little chums would follow, rather along the lines of those unlikely stories in the Sunday School prize-books, relics of my grandmother's childhood.

The encounter, when it happened, was rather a different experience. I was now a twenty-three-year-old wife and mother, home on leave from Aden. Erddig was only a short distance away from R's parents' house in Wrexham, where we had a flat. The park seemed just the place to take my son, aged one, out for a walk. The day was wet as usual and the drive down past the lodge (more derelict than ever) was rutted with mud. But we were both enjoying the scenery until an angry shout rang out.

'Didn't you see it?'

'Sorry?' I called.

'See the sign, of course!' A mad-looking figure in a long raincoat was coming towards us from under the trees waving a stick, a dog at his heels. I recognised the ageing Simon Yorke. 'The sign that says No Wheeled Vehicles!'

The stick was now being poked in the direction of the perambulator, an ancient black model borrowed from a neighbour. Interested in this disturbance, a small face peered out from under the hood.

'Yarg!' declared Howard. It was a favourite new word. The Squire was not amused.

'Surely – ' I began in dignified protest, drawing on my new role as a memsahib. But it was the wrong approach. Mr Yorke was red-faced with fury.

'Walkers, yes! Wheeled vehicles, no!' he barked. 'Do I make myself clear?'

I was still determined to end this confrontation on a reasonable note.

'I was just wondering where you get to if you come out on the other side of the park,' I said conversationally.

'But you're not "coming out on the other side".' The

Squire's voice quivered with indignation at the mere idea. 'You're going back the way you came! Now!' An afterthought struck him. 'Anyway, you'd only find yourself at Wynnstay.'

It was strangest of all to learn that, in Simon's mind, nothing existed between himself and the next great house several miles away. As in some seventeenth-century map, all the intervening landmarks of villages, housing estates and collieries had not yet been built.

After this, I could only accept defeat. Besides, the elderly terrier was now baring its teeth at me. The expression on the face of its owner was equally unsociable. Was there some atavistic echo of my South Wales forebears, I wondered, (especially Ben John, the gamekeeper) as I meekly obeyed the squirearchal command? At least I wasn't obliged to walk away backwards, which would have been difficult with a pram. Apparently anyone absent-mindedly taking a car into the grounds was made to drive back in reverse gear for the length of the park.

As I passed the lodge I was able to spot the famous notice-board, face-down in the grass . . . Not surprisingly, Erddig was thereafter dismissed from my mind. Then one day, many years later, I dropped into a familiar Wrexham saleroom, a ramshackle building under a railway bridge, a place to discover treasure if you were lucky. Having just moved into Hafod, I was on the look-out for household oddments rather than antiques. A large box labelled 'Mixed Lot' looked a possibility. There seemed to be things like table-cloths lurking beneath. So I joined in the bidding, but quickly dropped out. The hideous lampshade on top, patterned with goldfish, had put me off my stroke. So I let the box go to a tubby bespectacled man who got the lot for a fiver.

Someone behind me chuckled. 'You never know what the Squire'll go for.'

Before I could take this in, the successful bidder was at my side, beaming apologetically.

'I say, it was only the lampshade I wanted,' he confided in

a soft courteous voice. 'But if there's something in there you're after, you're welcome to have a look. I'm Phil Yorke, by the way, Simon's brother.'

This was so hard to believe, I was not sure how to respond. I was also trying to envisage what place there would be for a cracked plastic lampshade in ancestral Erddig.

I was able to see for myself soon enough. After presenting me with a maroon chenille tablecloth, the amiable Mr Yorke insisted on giving me a lift back to Llangollen. He was due at a church meeting in the next village, so it was no trouble. There was a slight hiatus while I was inserted into the back of the Austin Mini. The doors were tied up with twine and the front seat had been removed to make space for a load of slates. There was just room for a small black and white mongrel called Trixie to wedge herself against Philip's knees, and we were off down the High Street.

'On the way we can stop at Erddig,' he called over his shoulder. 'Do you know the house . . . ?'

Stopping at Erddig was my passport to this chaotic and magical kingdom which I was soon to know so well. It was also the start of a memorable friendship. Sadly the new Squire, a bachelor like Simon, seemed fated to be the last. This and more he explained to me, over the rattle of the engine as we turned in through the dark tanglewoods of beech and elm. He inherited the estate on his brother's death in 1966. Now he was determined to 'hold the fort' against all the odds.

'You'll see how it is,' he said simply. 'Simon did rather let things go.'

It was one of Philip's more striking understatements. The dignified classical front of the house gave no hint of the scenes of decline and fall within. But this was not what struck me first. To me it seemed a place of fantasy, of weird and wonderful eccentricity, breathing its secret history through every pore of those damp and peeling interiors. The way we went in was as strange as what lay ahead. It was a tiny basement entrance at the back of the house. Inside, the first door stood open. Judging from the clutter, this was Philip's kitchen, cornflakes, sliced bread, tinned milk and other iron rations scattered over the long table.

'This is the really important room,' he said. 'It's the old Servants' Hall, but the only servants left are up on the walls.'

I turned to the shadowy faces peering down from the cobwebs. It seems that in the 1790s the first Philip Yorke commissioned a series of portraits of his best workers, indoors and out, adding some catchy verses to each canvas to describe their roles at Erddig.

'His successors kept up the tradition so over the centuries there's almost a complete household record,' said Phil with a touch of pride.

It was the first inkling I had of the Yorkes' extraordinarily close relationship with their staff over the centuries, something that must have seemed odd indeed to their grandee neighbours. But there was only time for a glimpse of these stalwart characters, caught at their tasks by the artist as if by the camera – Edward Prince, the carpenter ('Good Chips from the Old Block'), William Williams, the blacksmith at his anvil, the witch-like Jane Ebbrell, 'Spider-Brusher to the Master', and the dashing negro coachboy in scarlet and gold, his brass horn over his shoulder.

> Pray Heaven may stand his present friend,
> Where, black or white, distinctions end.

So the first Philip had written in a commemoration poem.

But now the present-day Philip was hurrying ahead, still carrying his lampshade. I had the impression of a subterranean passageway hung with bells, a warren of different doors on either side with peeling labels still attached ... Lamp Room, Still Room, Flower Room, Butler's Pantry, Family Museum. But what could be meant by the one that read Tribes?

'The Royal Tribes of Wales,' Philip said briefly. 'One of the

Yorkes wrote a book about them, had the billiard-room decorated with their heraldic emblems.'

It was enough to be going on with, I suppose. The Squire was more interested in the array of empty dog-food tins piled up on a table at the end.

'Part of my security system.' He showed me the piece of string that was hooked onto the bolt of the outside door. 'We'd soon hear that lot crashing down if anyone tried to get in, wouldn't we, Trixie?'

But Trixie was making for the stairs.

'She wants to show you our other alarm.'

Halfway up, he placed a careful foot on the step above and looked pleased at the sound of a shrill ringing. This particular device involved two pieces of metal foil and a torch battery, hidden beneath the carpet.

'It certainly works when people come to stay,' he told me cheerfully.

So this new squire was no recluse, I thought, as we moved on into a once-elegant drawing-room. Two visitors' books lay open on the Georgian desk, alongside a .22 rifle and some cartridges. The firing-pin had been removed, he told me reassuringly. A camp bed and blankets and an overflowing suitcase were piled underneath.

But now Philip was busy fixing his lampshade onto a sideways-leaning standard lamp. He stood back to admire the effect.

'You have electricity then?' I asked him.

'Sometimes. The generator's in the back kitchen. I have to jump up and down a bit on the starting-handle. A dash of petrol over the ignition and it goes quite well. I say!' he went on gleefully. 'You must come in the evening next time. We'll have an Erddig Entertainment!'

His chubby pink face clouded for a moment as he looked around.

'Of course, there's still an awful lot to be done. Money's the problem. The estate hasn't been paying its way for ages.'

Once again he was disappearing ahead of me like the White Rabbit. Did I imagine it or were the floorboards actually moving underfoot as I followed him from one grand room to the next?

'Subsidence,' Philip said. The local colliery had been mining under the foundations for years, so the whole balance of the house had shifted. 'At night it's like being on board ship, timbers creaking, groans from the panelling. People think the place is haunted, but the only ghost anyone's seen is a Victorian butler. One died under chloroform having an operation, they say, poor fellow.'

The door into the dining-room seemed to be stuck. 'Same problem,' said Philip, giving it a shove with his shoulder.

Inside, once again, it was hard to take in the bizarre combination of splendour and decay. Glittering pier-glasses lined the walls, encrusted with gilded gesso. There were tattered curtains of the original crimson damask, silver-framed chairs with torn upholstery, exquisite chandeliers poised beneath cracked and peeling ceilings. Amongst the disorder of piled-up packages and papers, every dusty surface held treasures – eighteenth-century blue porcelain, engraved goblets, Chinese *famille rose* vases and delicate Chelsea figures.

'Rich Uncle John,' said Phil. This was the hard-headed John Mellor, a Master in Chancery, who took over the house from a bankrupt high sheriff in 1716, furnished it in the finest taste of the period and left it on his death to his nephew, the first Simon Yorke.

The smug countenance of Master Mellor looked down at us from under his full-bottomed wig with something like distaste. Next to him was an altogether more charming presence, a red-haired young woman called Anne Jemima. But it was her handsome brother, the first Philip Yorke, who dominated the room. Antiquarian and poet, friend of Garrick, the portrait by Gainsborough paid special attention to the lace ruffles at the wrists and the gold-topped cane.

Standing beneath his ancestors Philip was an incongruous

figure in his old blue suit and sandals. The thick spectacles and neatly-parted silvery hair gave him the look of a retired schoolmaster. Only the hands gave him away, purple with outdoor work, and scarred with many a misplaced hammer-blow. Even now he was concentrating on turning out his pockets, sorting through a jumble of nails and string and some scribbled scraps of paper.

Sounds from the next room distracted him.

'Oh dear!' I heard him call. 'The gardeners are here!'

I had a picture of a few faithful retainers struggling to keep the borders in order. I had yet to realize that at Erddig the gardeners were a flock of tame sheep. Their main task was to keep down the grass. Today though, lured by the open doors, they had made their way from the terrace into the Saloon, where they were hopefully grazing the threadbare Axminster.

'I'm afraid they've done it before,' said Philip. 'They can't resist the glass.'

Already one of them was butting irritably at its reflection in the long mirror where a large crack still awaited repair. There was a stern roll-call of the invaders – 'Posy! Merrylegs! Penelope!' – as Trixie saw them off the premises.

Philip glanced at his watch. 'Would you like a quick look upstairs before we go? I expect you've heard of the famous State Bed. So called because it's in such a state,' he added with a rueful smile.

The joke faded at the melancholy sight of the ornate four-poster now laid out with basins and chamber-pots to catch the leaks from the ceiling. The silk canopy hung in shreds and Mellor's Chinese wallpaper had long ago given up the ghost. Across the way in what had once been the Red Bedroom, I felt a different sadness. The sprightly young Anne Jemima died here of consumption at the age of sixteen. As Philip told me this, he showed me the bed designed for nursing her, the ratchets and handle that could raise or lower the head, and turn the mattress to one side.

Somehow the girl with red hair still seemed to be with us, flitting ahead up the narrow stairs that led to the attics. Before she became ill, perhaps she had amused herself up here with the maidservants, going through the trunks of out-of-date finery discarded by earlier generations of Yorke ladies. Now the passages were lined with buckets and hip-baths to collect the rain water which dripped relentlessly in. It was a house with a broken back, as Philip put it. One end of it had actually dropped five feet below the original foundation line. However soon the coal might run out and the mining come to an end, the damage was already done. In the meantime he was carrying on doggedly with his own first-aid system, patching the roof in the worst places, rigging up hosepipes to run down from the gutters, even out through the windows.

'It's helped a bit. Not *all* the bedrooms are leaking.' He was opening various doors as we went down again. Through one of them I caught sight of a recumbent figure under a quilt.

'It's only Hoo-Ha, always sleeps in late. He's usually in the Night Nursery. Likes to try each room in turn.'

As always, this was not the moment for further enlightenment. It was time for us to be on our way and the journey into Llangollen had other distractions. But within a few weeks I was to meet Hoo-Ha face to face. Alias Bertram Heyhoe, he was an old actor friend from the days when Philip was embarked on a somewhat shaky career in repertory. As it happened the occasion was a suitably theatrical one. In the Erddig tradition Phil had decided to entertain the visiting judge of assize, with Hoo-Ha cast in the role of butler. Sir William Mars-Jones, an extrovert Welshman, had been an enthusiastic actor himself in his undergraduate days. Rising to the occasion he arrived in knee-breeches and court jacket to take his place at the long scrubbed table in the Servants' Hall. The rest of us, a maverick solicitor friend, a distinguished historian and family, had done our best to strike the right balance between the formal and the impromptu. Philip had even donned his demob suit in honour of the judge. Happily he surveyed the faces gathered beneath the oil lanterns that hung from the beams.

'Now then! What are we going to eat?'

The servants of the past gazed unhelpfully down from the walls. But Hoo-Ha had everything under control. Howard and Vanessa had been dispatched to the local Chinese take-away and soon an array of chop-sueys, spare ribs and egg foo-yung were set before us. Almost enough cutlery was found in a corner cupboard (which also released a shower of yellowing bills). Grace was said by the youthful Adam Mars-Jones, acting as judge's marshal, and a bottle of madeira made its appearance, dusty as any stage-prop. This was something of a biblical miracle. Philip was a strict teetotaller with a particular fondness for Tizer cherryade. Later on, a second madeira was found, a Christmas present from an archdeacon's widow, so the company was in animated spirits by the time our host led us up to the reception rooms.

But it was the spell of Erddig that intoxicated us. With Philip ahead of us, lamp in hand, we wound our way back into an enchanted time-warp. In the drawing-room, the glow of a dozen candelabra produced a transformation. The grim spectre of rack and ruin retreated into the shadows. Silver salvers, newly polished, were gleaming along the walls. Every mirror reflected the flickering light. Even the figures on the tapestries seemed to be moving – or was it the usual Erddig draught stealing out from behind the lacquered screens? As a final touch, a string of old gaslights had been draped around the marble chimney-piece. Even the standard lamp twinkled into brief life, coaxed by Philip's earlier efforts with the generator.

'And now, some after-dinner entertainment, I think.'

Bemused, we found ourselves in what was called the Entrance Hall. This was a room where the Yorkes always entertained guests in the evening we were told, chamber music in the early days, no doubt. But the family moved with the times. Victorian and Edwardian mechanical devices were ranged on every side. Like some sorcerer's apprentice, Phil dodged from one to the other, winding them up into life, so that soon they were all playing together – the Swiss musical box, the Parisian polyphone, the Thomas Edison phonograph. Even the Rheims Grand Forte had its own pianola, splendidly entitled 'the Metrostyle Threnodist Orchestrelle Company'. Once again we were snatched away into the past as these echoes of vanished gaieties filled the room, polkas and waltzes and trembling Puccini arias.

'This one was nearly the death of the rector of Marchwiel's daughter,' said Phil *sotto voce*. He had opened up something called a mandoline to show us the creakily revolving interior. 'There was a dance for someone's birthday. Apparently she went twirling by so close that the ribbons of her dress got caught up in the machinery and she was thrown into the fireplace. Luckily no fire, no harm done . . . '

Now it was the turn of this evening's guests. Sir William produced his guitar and was soon composing calypsos, undeterred by the scowling scrutiny of the red-robed Bloody Assize Judge Jeffreys in the Kneller portrait over his head. R gave us some boogie-woogie on the nineteenth-century Gothic organ. Finally, by popular request, Phil sat down to play his musical saw, leading us in his favourite songs.

'Let the Rest of the World Go By' somehow seemed to catch the true Erddig spirit, lingering on as we made our departures by lantern-light, into the snow.

Often enough Philip would appear out of the blue at Hafod to carry me off on other diversions. There was the skating party with none of us, even the Marquess of Anglesey, able to stay upright on the frozen lake for more than five minutes in our borrowed skates. Phil had unearthed a forgotten hoard from a trunk in the boathouse, dating back to the First World War.

'Nothing wrong with them! Just a bit rusty!'

At other times he would be visited by old friends from his early days. One-time actors like Heyhoe, they would enjoy reliving the glories of the Country Theatre Players, a 1920s company based in a bus at Bexhill-on-Sea. Dog-eared photograph albums were passed around.

'I don't think I was what you'd call a matinée idol,' said Philip sadly. He was examining a blurred snapshot of himself as Second Chinese Servant in Somerset Maugham's *The Letter*. 'Not quite up to the first Philip Yorke.'

He reminded us of his ancestor's roles in the elegant country house theatricals at Wynnstay, produced by Garrick.

'It was in the blood though, wasn't it?' piped up an elderly actress with a new career in television.

Philip wasn't too sure. His rowing achievements at Cambridge seemed to point him in another direction. But then he enrolled for a future in holy orders, concentrating on church missionary work.

'And you still do a bit of lay preaching, don't you?' prompted someone else.

'Then there was that taxi-service he used to run to Spain,' Heyhoe reminded us.

More and more pieces of Philip's life kept falling out of the conversation like a jigsaw-puzzle that was impossible to put together again.

But now, 'and for the rest of my life', it was Erddig that demanded all his energies and devotion. This was something we saw for ourselves whenever we were enrolled into one of his working parties.

As we arrived, Philip would be glimpsed as a face beaming up at us through the bars of the basement scullery like a happy convict. The face would be wreathed in shaving soap as this was where he liked to conduct his morning *toilette*. Later, painting window-frames alongside R, there was the chance of a chat about life at Bow Street. Philip had a special interest in this court, he told us, something to do with a cycling offence while he was living in London.

'Apparently it was against the law to hold onto the back of a lorry to get up a bit of speed on the old bike,' he said wonderingly. 'I told them I might well have been helping to push it along, but I don't think they believed me. Two and six the Beak fined me, would you believe it!'

Making lists in the library was my own assignment. Howard, meanwhile, had been taken on as a 'live-in' handyman ensconced in a tiny cottage called Bryn Goleu. Harry and Fred, two of the last estate workers, gave him some brisk instruction in slating and sawing. But most of the time he was with Philip, helping with various tasks which might include loading up the family silver into the Austin Mini for delivery to the bank, or resurrecting a favourite motorbike from the stables.

'Fearless he is!' Harry would say, as they watched him take the ancient tractor on a short cut through the river. 'And you should see him up on that roof!' Howard's only problem was to get him to sit still long enough for him to finish his portrait of the Last Squire.

Throughout this time there was the underlying sense of a major drama developing. The rumours came and went. The Historic Buildings Council had offered to repair the furniture. The National Coal Board proposed compensation for the structural damage. Most importantly, the National Trust were interested in acquiring the house. With the new building boom, the sale of Erddig land would provide the Trust with an endowment of over a million, more than sufficient persuasion to take on a property that preserved three centuries of history intact.

But would Philip agree to the takeover? Any discussion with officialdom was completely foreign to his nature. Talk of wills and trusts and grants aroused confusion and suspicion. His worst fear was the possible dispersal of the family possessions, the break-up of the home he'd loved all his life.

'What will happen to me? I suppose they'll put me behind glass like a period curiosity.'

He shook his head, still undecided. He'd turned up at Hafod in his unexpected way, bearing muffins for tea and an Edwardian lady's bicycle-bag. This was now upturned on the parlour carpet to let loose an avalanche of papers. On his knees, he spread them out between us, old letters, diaries, notepads, exercise-books.

'Just some personal stuff about Erddig, mostly my own jottings since I took over. You may find my writing a bit of a problem but I expect you'll manage.' He looked at me hopefully over his glasses.

It suddenly dawned on me that I had been appointed as some kind of archivist. My heart sank as I surveyed the hundreds of smudged and crumpled pages.

'But these are private papers,' I said feebly.

'Oh, they'll be safe enough with you,' was his reply.

Touched as I was, intensely curious as I was, I knew I would have to turn down the idea. Apart from the responsibility, the material would take months to transcribe and a professional typist would be needed. In the meantime I had radio commitments to keep and a novel to finish.

Phil seemed to understand.

'Never mind,' he said cheerfully, stuffing it all back into the bag. 'You can always take a look at them next time you're at Erddig.'

But next time was to be a different kind of day altogether, a day spent recording a radio programme to mark the forthcoming handover of Erddig to the National Trust. Some months earlier Phil phoned to let us know the news. He had finally signed the deed of gift. 'It's for the best.' He sounded half-wary, half-jubilant. 'There's a splendid young man from the Trust called Merlin Waterson. He's in charge of the whole restoration business, got all the right ideas.'

And so here I was with tape recorder, producer and engineer, walking through the old rooms that were no longer quite so familiar now they were back in their original glory, rescued in the nick of time by an army of craftsmen and other experts. All of a sudden it seemed a daunting task to package into forty-five minutes of air-time the unique character of the place and its owners.

But Philip made it easy. Back in his thespian mode he spun the stories together in his own seemingly artless fashion. Right at the start I asked him what was the sound that conjured up his earliest memories of the house. For answer he turned and drew back the huge old shutters in the Saloon, one after the other. The distant creakings and rumblings told a child it was morning, as the servants opened up the house for the day.

After that, the programme was launched on its way. But, being Philip, he was to provide us with one unscheduled moment of drama. A few years earlier he and I had found ourselves locked in the family chapel while he showed me around this strangely gloomy addition to the house. Only prolonged calls and the ringing of a muffin-bell brought Heyhoe to our rescue. Once again we were on our own in the chapel, this time with microphones attached.

'It could easily happen again,' said Philip. He was wearing that impish grin of his. 'The listeners would find it exciting, don't you think?'

Apparently they did. So did the television crew who were above us filming the restoration of the State Bed. The bells and thumps and cries for help were too much for an engineer called Mike who'd retired for a lie-down. 'He's the psychic one,' said his friend. 'Said the place was haunted right from the start.'

A few months later Philip provided us with one last moment of suspense. We knew he was always unpredictable. Even so neither R nor I were prepared for the bombshell that was delivered to Hafod by Philip himself. It was about eight o'clock in the morning. Through the bedroom window we could see a familiar figure pacing the gravel path.

'Hope I didn't wake you,' he said in his usual polite way. 'But I needed to talk. Rather urgent, you see.'

He seemed distressed. We urged him into the kitchen for some breakfast. Only then did the announcement come.

'I'm thinking of withdrawing!'

'Withdrawing?'

'Taking Erddig back from the Trust, while there's still time.'

But surely there wasn't 'still time'. In just six weeks Erddig was to be officially opened to the public by the Prince of Wales. What on earth could have gone wrong?

In between the toast and marmalade and several mugs of strong tea, the doubts came tumbling out. He had betrayed his family. It was nothing to do with Merlin, but The National Trust had become The National Distrust. Their official history of Erddig reflected the Yorkes in a bad light. The proposed tour of the house was untrue to the Yorke traditions. Now that a curator had been installed, his own role was non-existent. It had been suggested he live in one of the terraced houses in the town that was part of the estate.

'Not that I mind the house.' He brightened. 'There's a jolly good fish and chip shop just opposite. It's just the principle.'

Another worry had arisen. What would he wear at this opening ceremony?

There was a simple answer. The famous Demob Suit was still intact. What was wrong with that?

We followed up with more serious reassurances. The prospect of the glorious resurrection of Erddig would surely delight the souls of deceased Yorkes who were so proud of their home. Anyway, what was the alternative for an estate with no heirs?

'I could always get married.' There was a note of desperation this time. 'It's still not too late.' Another pause.

'Besides, I did think at one time of leaving it to the Welsh Nationalists.'

In a final effort, I tried a tactic that might appeal to a one-time player with the Bexhill Repertory.

'I think it's just stage-fright,' I said. 'Once you're up there on the platform making your speech, everything will be fine.'

'Besides,' added R, 'you can't let Prince Charles down.'

By the time he left us, Philip had seen sense. At any rate, there was no more talk of withdrawal. The great day dawned, breezy but fine. Philip's speech, delivered from a rustic pavilion, was a model of courtly charm, sprinkled with tales of the Yorke royal connections – the ancestress who had been a lady-in-waiting to Queen Anne, George III's praise of the Erddig woods and, of course, the visit of Queen Mary who was especially taken with the painted motto in the kitchen, 'Waste Not Want Not'. ('I wish my staff would remember that!')

Then with a bow, the Squire presented the Prince with a watch given to his grandmother by Queen Victoria.

'Hope it's still ticking, Sir!' Then, holding it to his ear with a smile of triumph – 'It's OK! The police got it to go this morning!'

The air of celebration mounted. The royal guest of honour fell off the Erddig penny-farthing without injuring himself. The Rhos Silver Band played 'God Bless the Prince of Wales'. Throngs of the gentry and the county, the celebrities and the tenants, mingled under the bunting with Wrexham trade and mayoralty. Some very old ladies were enjoying being pushed around in their wheelchairs. Philip had gone through the visitors' books from the turn of the century to add every possible name to the list. Amidst the cheers and the congratulations he suddenly realised he had the Erddig party of a lifetime on his hands.

'I say! Don't go, everyone,' I heard him call, rushing from group to group. 'You must come through the house! See what's been done!'

But I had to leave. I had someone to meet at the station. Besides, just for a while, I wanted to keep the old crazy Erddig clear in my mind before it was overlaid by this fine phoenix risen from the ashes of the past.

A Ram in the Well

I caught a farewell wave from Philip as he was carried away by his guests. Then the scene faded. I was reminded of the receding horizon of so many South Sea farewells. Just as strongly, I had the sense that there would be no return to this particular Eden either . . .

11

CALLING ON MRS ROBERTS

At Hafod the seasons produced their own transformation scenes. Hay-cutting and sheep-shearing, the August bank holiday fête and Gathering the Mountain in October are all familiar sign-posts on the journey through the seasons. Time in the valley is circular and makes life seem changeless. But there was one festival on the calendar that could not last forever and for that very reason was all the more venerated with every passing year. Mrs Morgan Roberts's birthday had, in fact, become a kind of Welsh Thanksgiving.

Looking across from Hafod, despite the rain-clouds I had a bird's-eye view of Pant Glas farm, almost as good as the buzzards', who seemed to be wheeling and piping over the valley with particular enthusiasm that morning. Since breakfast time there had been what amounted to a traffic jam up and down the twisting lanes. Under his black umbrella the minister from Bethesda Chapel was an early visitor, bearing the good wishes of Presbyterian deacons and elders from the surrounding districts, no doubt. After that, the farm dogs kept up a constant chorus as the muddy cars and ancient Land Rovers and even a tractor or two tangled together bringing friends and relations and other well-wishers to the house. Elaborate bouquets were delivered from Mrs Hughes's 'Belles-Fleurs' establishment in Llangollen. Dewi the Post made a special late call to be sure of the last-minute birthday cards and to give himself time for a celebratory cup of tea and a slice of Gwyneth's famous fruit-cake.

Halfway into her nineties, Mrs Roberts must have grown well accustomed to such visitations and indeed seemed to flourish on them. Even so, I decided to wait a day or two before I made my own pilgrimage to Pant Glas. Ever since that first foray of mine to catch the Why-Walk bus, I had imagined that the climb would get easier with practice. But it never did. On my way up to the road there were many breathless halts for a quick chat with Gwyneth or her mother, always with the promise to come in for a 'proper visit' next time.

So this was the proper visit. It had been raining, off and on, for some days, not the horizontal *niwl* but the steady vertical stuff, so there was no point in waiting. Slowed down with boots and umbrella and a bottle of sherry (Mrs Roberts liked a sip now and then for 'the medicinal') it took me longer than usual. I was almost there, only to be stopped in my tracks by the sight of a maroon-coloured pantechnicon veering down the lane towards me, half-hidden by trees. For a wild moment I thought it was a return visit from Rhys the Remove. Then, to my relief, it turned off through the farm gates and I could see the imposing logo of the Denbighshire County Council, a dragon rampant on top of a castle, with the legend 'Llyfrgell Deithiol'. The mobile library was making its monthly round of the valleys, just in time to supply Mrs Roberts with some restful reading after the social demands of the last few days.

With spray flying up from the wheels, it rocked to a halt in the yard. The dogs had been tied up but half a dozen hens gathered round expectantly as the door slid open and a small ladder was let down. Finally the curly red head of the

Mobile Librarian emerged, one Eifion Jones, better identified as Jones the Books.

'Hafod, isn't it?' he called out to me. 'Coming aboard?'

I hesitated. What was the correct order of precedence, the library or Mrs Roberts? The problem was solved when Mrs R herself appeared in the porchway. A favourite plaid shawl round her shoulders, she was holding out a basket of books.

'Tell Eifion I didn't like this last lot,' she instructed me in her usual piercing quaver. 'Especially the Lloyd George. Disgraceful it was!'

Inside the van, Eifion was now tucked behind a small folding counter. He grinned as he inspected the book in question.

'*Dearest Pussy* – LG's letters to his mistress, aren't they? I should have known better. Never mind.' He began rummaging through a box at his feet. 'I've got just the thing for her somewhere.'

I asked him if he selected for all his customers.

'Not all. But I've got to know what they like best.' He waved his hand round at the shelves that were stacked from roof to floor. 'Agatha Christie, Sherlock Holmes, Dick Francis, they're the favourites. And then there's Romance. A widow up the *bwlch* gets through ten Barbara Cartlands a month. Must be reliving her youth!'

Other clients had arrived on my heels. Two tiny ladies in pixie-hoods, the retired postmistress and her friend, were shaking off mackintosh capes and settling down to browse among the science fiction. An ancient nut-brown man in cycling shorts was searching for *Yoga For The Over-Sixties* while a hoarse voice at the window wanted to know if *Welsh Fairies and Phantoms* had arrived yet.

'That's for Mrs Mostyn-Price, the Plas,' Eifion confided. 'Mad on the supernatural, she is. Always sends her husband to collect for her!'

'You could do with an assistant,' I told him, as he stamped a hasty choice of mine.

'I did have one,' he told me. 'Mair Prytherch from Corwen. Only lasted a week though. Said the motion of the springs made her that seasick, even four Kwells first thing didn't help. Worse than the Holyhead ferry, she said it was.'

I reached for the handrail. With the rain lashing down and the wind gusting across us from side to side there was certainly a nautical feeling about the Mobile even when stationary. I felt some sympathy for Miss Prytherch.

'Mind you, it's worse in bad weather,' Eifion added.

'Bad weather?' I was wrestling on the steps with a half-open umbrella.

'The snow. Had to get Will's tractor to drag me out two winters ago and then he went straight into the ditch behind me. No books out that day, I can tell you.' He reached under the counter. 'That reminds me. Something for Mrs Roberts. Tell her Happy Birthday from me.'

At the door, Gwyneth was waiting to welcome me, dressed for callers in neat tweed skirt and cardigan. She eyed the book in my hand. 'My mother will be pleased. She loves her big-print.'

'What did he send this time?' Mrs Roberts called from the parlour. As I went through to her the sight of the title produced a radiant smile. 'Well, well! The life of Ann Griffiths. The greatest of our Welsh hymn-writers, you know.'

She peered into my bag. 'And what did you get?'

I tried stalling. 'Another writer from Wales. Not hymns though.'

Too late. Mrs Roberts had already spotted the name. 'Jan Morris. The one you interviewed on the radio, isn't it? Used to be a man, then got turned into a woman.'

I was still thinking of the best way to change the subject but Mrs Roberts was unruffled. 'We had a cockerel did that. Changed sex, I mean.'

Coming in with a tray of tea, Gwyneth burst out laughing. 'It was the other way round, mam. Remember? The hen decided to be a cockerel because the old one had died.'

'Anyway, lot of fuss about nothing,' said Mrs Roberts. 'Lloyd George, now. That was a real scandal. Taking up with his secretary and everyone knowing about it.' She pursed her lips. 'Still, they say she helped him a lot with his work. So that's something.'

Tea was dispensed in rose-patterned cups, Mrs Roberts small and upright in her wing chair, white hair freshly waved, a cameo brooch pinned to her white lace collar. There was almost the atmosphere of visiting some venerable shrine with those banks of respectful flower arrangements, candles on the piano and, on every side, family photographs arrayed like holy pictures, from today's pink-faced cherubs to the saintly icons of sepia-coloured Victorians. The room was very warm. Mrs Roberts reached for the poker to stir the fire, indicating that another piece of coal should be placed on it. It was the moment for the sherry to be poured into three thimble-sized glasses.

Mrs Roberts took a reckless sip. 'We all need a little tonic from time to time.' She patted my hand with a conspiratorial smile.

Once again the talk turned to scandal, this time the long-dead sins of our own tiny village. It seemed that one-street Pandy, with its crumbling cottages and wandering sheep, had once been a hotbed of wickedness of every kind – drinking, brawling, loose living, the lot. That was in the heyday of the slate-mines up on the Pass when the quarrymen were a byword for their riotous ways. No wonder, I thought, after the appalling hazards of the daily shift in the bowels of the mountain, with water up to the waist and rockfalls from dynamite blasts that could kill a man without warning.

Until this moment, Pandy had always reminded me of Goldsmith's *Deserted Village*. Instead, listening to Mrs Roberts, ghosts from a Wild West scenario emerged, gunfights at the Last Chance Saloon of the village pub, holdups at the corner shop. Nowadays the old Bridge Inn was the neatly painted home of the district nurse and her mother. No children swarmed in and out of the red-brick school, which had been reinvented as something called the Community Centre. Even the post office-cum-local store was a thing of the past.

'It's hard to believe,' I said.

Mrs Roberts stabbed a crooked finger towards the desk in the corner.

'Better show her that old pamphlet,' she directed Gwyneth. 'The one Megan found in the drawer. Read her a bit of that.'

It was obvious that Gwyneth was almost as passionate a historian as her sister. '"January 1859,"' she began, respectfully unfolding the yellowing page close to her nose. '"Report of the Revivalist Movement in the village of Pandy in Denbighshire."' She paused only briefly as she translated from the Welsh. But the emotional rise and fall of the original still clung to her every syllable.

'"Meetings were held every night in the Bethesda Chapel. There was praying like steam but more effort was needed. Three weeks later Joseph Jones and William Morgan (Wesleyan) came to preach from Matthew 16, verse 26, on Losing One's Soul. It was as if a strong wind went running through the congregation. The worst sinners lost control, stamping and crying out 'What must I do to be saved? Give me shelter from the wrath to come!'"'

Pausing for breath, Gwyneth looked up at me. 'Don't worry. I shan't read it all.'

But I was caught up in the picture of the little chapel, bursting at the seams with wild-eyed converts. I wanted to hear the end of the story.

'So did they really change their ways?'

Gwyneth turned to the other side of the page. '"The Devil's Army is undone" is what it says there. "No less than seventy have enlisted for Jesus Christ. There is no drunkenness or swearing in the quarries now,"' she went on, '"the talk is all of religious matters, last Sunday's sermon, the words of the

Bible. Before the Revival these men behaved like animals. Now on pay-days and fair-days they come home tidy, in their right clothes and their right senses!"'

Mrs Roberts gave me something like a wink. 'All except Ned from the Hafod.'

Gwyneth cleared her throat for the final peroration. '"Brethren, there may be a fall from grace from time to time! But, in the name of the Lord, let us hope for strength and pray for salvation!"'

'Amen,' chirped Mrs Roberts, downing the last drop of sherry.

Was this the same chapel she went to every Sunday, I asked her.

She nodded, the only one in the district now. The Wesleyans closed theirs a long time ago. Just lately one had been converted to a place that sold beds. '"Seventh Heaven" they call it.' She snorted. 'Sounds like blasphemy to me.'

'My mother's still very strict,' Gwyneth murmured. 'There's no work allowed in her fields on a Sunday, have you noticed?'

Mrs Roberts had placed a small log on the fire and was gazing rather dreamily into the glow.

'In my young days,' she said, 'the best thing about Sundays was the courting.'

'Not in chapel, surely, Mrs Roberts?'

I was only teasing but she shot me a sharp glance. 'Afterwards I'm talking about. We were allowed to walk in pairs as far as the bridge. There was a bit of leaning on the rail for a chat, then home. We looked smart too, all of us in our best. Everyone went to chapel then from all around. And what a service it was, organ and everything. Pulled out all the stops with the singing too!'

There was a brief lull in the conversation. From the next room I was startled to hear what sounded like a reincarnation of those long-ago Sundays. A massed congregation seemed to have squeezed itself into the kitchen and was now launched into the opening verse of a well-known hymn. Two solo voices joined them, a soaring tenor and a rich bass.

'Owen and Will,' said Gwyneth. She got up to lead the way through. Sitting at each end of a long scrubbed table, the two brothers were beating time to the service that was crackling out from an ancient wireless on the dresser. As we went in, the hymn reached a crescendo but the two solo voices died away. Owen looked bashful.

'Sunday service from Bettws, it is. They repeat it on a Tuesday.'

Will helped himself to another piece of pork pie. 'Just getting in a bit of practice while we have our dinner. Cymanfa Ganu at Carrog this afternoon.'

As the leading lights of the North Denbighshire Male Voice Choir, the Davis brothers were expected to do the valley proud at this traditional singing festival. Both were dressed in best dark suits, Owen, a few years younger, fair-haired and strikingly handsome alongside Will's more weather-worn features.

'We were trying to remember if this was the old version or a new one,' said Owen as the hymn died away.

'Lloyd, it is,' said Will. 'I'm sure of it.'

'No, no. That one's the Howell,' Owen insisted, rather pink in the face. 'Eighteen-ninety-something, isn't it?'

Apparently, in Wales, the composer of the tune is more important than the writer of the words. So a hymn-book was brought out from the dresser drawer to decide the matter in Owen's favour.

Settled in her chair at the table watching Gwyneth cut up fresh ham sandwiches, Mrs Roberts was scornful. 'Your Great-uncle Elwyn would have known that without going to the book.'

'Probably would have sung it through too.' Will was laughing. 'Especially after a spot of the Oh-Be-Joyful.'

'Home brew,' Gwyneth explained. 'He used to make it in a

huge old wash-tub and the local constable was always the first to sample it.'

'Not a teetotaller was Uncle Elwyn,' Mrs Roberts admitted. 'Not a Methodist either, until the week before he died. Roman Catholic he was, until they told him about Purgatory.'

'And when he was a boy,' put in Owen, 'wasn't he the one who got pushed into a grave he was digging with the other lads, just for a joke?'

'Joke maybe,' Mrs Roberts said grimly. 'But that's when he got that bad stammer of his. Never lost it from that day on.'

'Family stories,' said Will, still laughing.

The two men got up to go. 'We'll have to risk Dilys,' Owen said.

Gwyneth reassured him she'd look out for her, and anyway the old thing was used to calving, wasn't she?

This prompted a fresh reminiscence. Remember the time their father let some gypsies sleep the night in the barn and next morning none of the calves would go near the place because of the smell of tobacco?

Cap in hand, Will stood in the doorway, reminded of something else.

'Indian pedlars used to come round in those days too,' he told me. 'Selling silks and stuff to the farmers' wives for weddings, they were. One day my mother let one of them have an old hen for a shilling, so I hid behind a tree to watch what he did with it.' Back behind that tree for a minute, Will screwed up his face like a small boy. 'First the old man took it down to the brook to wring its neck. Next he plucked it and washed it. And then he ate it raw, all in a few great swallows. That's the bit I can never forget.' He shook his head. 'Imagine how hungry he must have been.'

Owen brought out his watch from his waistcoat pocket. 'Come on then. We'll be late.'

With the two men gone, the three of us sat down to a dainty version of the sandwiches and pie. Mrs Roberts was still remembering gypsies, the vivid sight of them, so bright and foreign-looking in the green lanes. When she was a little girl the women used to dress her up in their shawls and necklaces and she enjoyed that.

'But you couldn't refuse them anything, in case you got cursed, like the old lady who used to live in the Hafod. She was milking a cow, she said, and the minute she turned the gypsies away, the milk stopped. Sent her husband after them fast to buy some pegs or there'd be no butter for market-day,' she said.

'And it worked?'

'Of course. Well that's the story, isn't it?'

The Welsh sermon from Bettws Chapel was still rising and falling in the background with a hypnotic sound like the brook under the bridge. Perhaps it was considered bad manners to switch off a minister in full flood. But now, on Mrs Roberts's suggestion, we were about to explore the house, something I had always longed to do. A famously old dwelling, it was rooted in the hollow of the valley with the little river at its feet and, rising above it, the slopes of King Offa's famous Dyke, built to confine the Welsh within their tribal boundaries. A maze of stone stables and outhouses encircled it. There was the granary too, still smelling of sacks of corn from the mill that was no more. Next to it was the barn where the new television aerial was precariously perched above a slit window brought from the abbey centuries ago.

But it was the house itself, a sprawling whitewashed affair, that was the heart of Pant Glas. Walking through, Mrs Roberts led the way, stick in hand, and as we walked, we talked – those non-stop Welsh flurries of conversation that distract the attention from everything else. In every room tiny details leapt out at me and were lost again. I followed them into the dairy called the *bwtri*. Among the cool-smelling slate slabs Mrs Roberts grasped the handle of the pulley that churned the butter and told me to look through the little window at where the horse used to go 'round and round' in the yard to turn it.

'Horses for everything then. Remember old Tommy?' she said to Gwyneth. 'That funny trick of his? Loved men's caps, he did. He'd snatch one off anyone's head, if he was standing near enough!'

The big shire horses always went ploughing in pairs and there was still an expression used to describe two different personalities, Gwyneth told me. A Lead Horse was one who liked the limelight. One who was reliable but shy was the Shaft Horse. 'Like in the WI,' she explained. 'There's the President, and there's the Treasurer. But, whatever the difference, they've got to work well together, haven't they?'

Mrs Roberts reached up to the line of milk-cans hanging on the wall and took down the smallest to show me. 'I used to take my dinner to school in this. Bread and milk it was and at the bottom my penny for the teacher, so that I didn't lose it.' She smiled wryly. 'Fancy paying someone who gave you the cane every time you spoke a word of Welsh. And you had a board hung round your neck too. The Welsh Not it was called – Welsh Not to be spoken in School, it said.' Shaking her head, she replaced the battered object on its nail. 'For our own good, they said it was. Welsh was to be stamped out in those days. But they didn't win in the end, did they?'

'It's the other way round now,' Gwyneth said. 'Everything's bilingual and why not? This is Wales, after all, isn't it?'

By now we've moved into the old working kitchen where the warmth from the range revives memories of bacon sides hanging from hooks, pipe-tobacco, wet boots, hot loaves in the bread oven. Brought in for the winter, red geraniums crowd the window ledge. Here and there the slab floors are worn into hollows. The dogs drink buttermilk from them though no one explains why. In the passageway a patch of wall has been left uncovered to show crumbs of the first mud and wattle under the plaster. Under one of the beams someone has cut the date, 1693, with the last figure the wrong way round. Next to it is an exquisitely carved sunflower flanked by the initials EP, thought to be one Elwyn Price of about the same time.

'One of my grandsons is a wood-carver in London,' Mrs Roberts tells me. 'Better than old EP, though. Working at Hampton Court he was, last year.'

The oak staircase creaks under its polish. Halfway up a door bangs and makes us jump.

'Only a window left open,' Gwyneth reassures us. She shows me the way the door closes with its old drop-latch. 'And a bolt on the outside! We always wondered about that. Like the wife in *Jane Eyre*, Megan always says. She's the reader in this family is Megan.'

The open window fails to make the upstairs rooms any colder than they already are. There's a spartan touch about farm bedrooms in Wales with their pale green paint and bleak overhead lights. No one needs cosseting here, the bedrooms say, not after all that hard work and mountain air.

Mrs Roberts's room has a touch of luxury though, a feather bed with a pink satin quilt and a lace spread to go over it.

'We thought you might like to see these,' Gwyneth says, opening the wardrobe door. Inside hangs a row of spectral shapes, Victorian best dresses worn by Mrs Roberts's grandmother who refused to throw them away even when they were no longer in use. 'We're putting together a few old things to raise money for the Sunday School Eisteddfod,' Gwyneth explains.

'"Exhibition of Local Antiquities" Megan's calling it, family photographs, bits of pottery, fossils, farming things from the old days, that kind of thing. Sounds a bit posh but I think people might be interested. And these are history in a way, aren't they?'

Treasure, I call it, as, one by one, the dresses are brought out. There's the pungent whiff of mothballs with a hint of lavender, as they rustle stiffly on their hangers. The bunchy skirts are short – 'she was small like the old Queen,' Mrs Roberts tells me. Some are lined with taffeta and some with Welsh flannel and all are black.

'Black,' Mrs Roberts sighs. 'I never like to wear it, do you? It's not just the funerals –'

She breaks off. But Gwyneth picks up the thread of a horrifying story that belongs to the same era. In those days village girls often went into service with wealthy Liverpool families, to be able to send money home to their families in Wales. There was consternation when one unfortunate girl – Mari Griffiths – was sent home suffering from a mysterious fever, her body horribly swollen and black. Perhaps, with folk memories of the Black Death, the rumour went round that it was some kind of plague, perhaps a disease spread from abroad at the docks. Whatever the explanation, Mari was sent home to die and die she did. The family house was given a wide berth by the local people and very few came to the funeral, though Mrs Roberts's grandfather volunteered to be one of the bearers. Only later did the terrible truth emerge. The girl had scalded herself with boiling oil and was too scared to tell her employers.

Her voice hushed, Mrs Roberts took up the tale. 'They said it was from her black stockings that the infection had spread. Right through her whole body, poor *bach*. So what killed her was blood poisoning, and no cure for that in those days, was there?' She looked down at the dresses spread around us on the white counterpane. 'I still think of it, somehow, whenever I see black.'

There is something so melancholy and so grotesque about this account that the three of us sit in silence for a moment. Then, briskly, Gwyneth becomes the practical hostess again, switching the light on and drawing the curtains against the rainy dusk. Mrs Roberts decides to have a bit of a lie-down with Ann Griffiths, so I make my farewells and Gwyneth ushers me downstairs.

A Ram in the Well

'I never asked if you needed to use the bathroom – the *ty bach*, that is,' she says, adding her little joke. 'It's inside nowadays, don't worry.'

I gathered that, not all that long ago, the 'little house' was some twenty yards across the yard, a solid construction of slate and stone, disguising the usual earth-closet. And that was the one for visitors. The everyday one was the far side of the field, no joke when you were carrying a lantern in freezing snow or rain.

Could it be worse than the Fijian toads, I wonder. With some relish, I describe to Gwyneth the problems of staying in a strange village and finding your way to the lean-to in the mangroves while the glare of the hurricane lamp brought these Pacific monsters leaping out to greet you every step of the way.

Down in the kitchen, Megan wants to know why we are laughing. She is waiting to deliver a letter from their niece in Spain, Bethan's daughter, Kate, who sends news home every week to be circulated around the entire family, starting with Mrs Roberts, of course. In the doorway is Aled and another of Bethan's sons called David. Aled has a gun over his arm and a pair of rabbits swinging from his hand – 'for Nain's favourite stew'. David has come to help with the milking, with both Will and Owen away – a rare occasion.

It's stopped raining, so Megan says she'll walk up the hill with me. As we reach the gate, a plaintive moan from the barn floats through the mist like a foghorn.

'I'll leave you to it,' Megan calls back to Gwyneth.

There are lights shining out from another farm, just above the village. 'That's one of ours too,' Megan tells me. 'Bryn and his family are there. It's got a very old weathervane over the porch. I always remember when I was little my mother used to take me up for a Sunday walk "to see the wind".'

As always, I'm aware of the richness of this close-knit way of life. I find myself almost envious of such continuity, such a powerful sense of identity, compared with my own relations' somewhat tenuous links with each other, suspended between half a dozen different backgrounds from rural Pembrokeshire to the industrial north.

The dogs are, of course, the essential lower orders of the human tribe. One of them is following now at our heels, the wall-eyed Pero, his nose bent to decipher the latest trail of sheep droppings. As if reading my thoughts, Megan says, 'I suppose you think Pero's a typical farm dog, never been off the mountain. But I'll tell you a secret.'

'As long as he doesn't mind.'

We stop for a breather and Pero is eyeing us both, ears cocked at the mention of his name.

'Well, a couple of years ago my Auntie Mair moved out of the valley into a nice little house in the town. Her husband had died and she took Pero with her for company. He didn't like the traffic one bit and we all thought he'd never settle. Then one weekend Auntie Mair went away to a wedding so Will brought him back to the farm for a couple of days. And what do you think?'

Pero waits intently and so do I.

'The very night she was back she was woken up by Pero barking to be let in. It was four o'clock in the morning. He'd walked the five miles from the farm, down the main road, through the Llangollen streets and there he was outside the front door, if you please, as if it was the most normal thing in the world. Seems he'd turned into a town dog after all.'

I put my hand on Pero's bony head. 'He's back with you on the farm again, though?'

'Well, sadly, Auntie Mair died last year so there was nothing else for him but back to work. Seems quite happy about it, so he must be good at adapting.' She laughs. 'Bit like you with your London trips for the BBC.'

Pero's expression is rather smug, I think, as we exchange glances.

'Best of both worlds,' he seems to be saying. 'If you know how.'

12

A DOUBLE LIFE

It was all very well for Pero, I thought. He only had to trot a few miles down a country road to exchange one way of life for another. My two worlds were such poles apart I almost had to change personality to bridge them. Arriving in London on one of those back-to-work expeditions of mine, I never quite knew what challenges *Woman's Hour* would have in store for me. It might be a live programme from the Ideal Home Exhibition – a surreal contrast to the Hafod domestic scene – or a studio discussion about breast-feeding – or ballooning – or Elizabeth Barrett Browning. It might even be an interview with the King of Tonga on one of his visits to renew a long-standing friendship with the Queen. Whatever the plans, Broadcasting House, W1, would certainly deliver a severe shock to the system to someone who had been dwelling in a Rousseau-esque state of innocence on a wild Welsh mountain.

The hazards of this double life began with the journey down. This was always an obstacle race in itself, especially in the depths of winter. The cruel uprooting started at dawn with the struggle to get water to flow from frozen pipes, a kettle to be boiled on a reluctant fire if, as so often, the power had been mysteriously cut off in the night. Outside the window, the valley was swathed in a dense fog.

Would I make it? Waiting for the last of my stale cornflakes, the robin eyed me through the glass, piping tunelessly of the folly of human endeavour.

Inevitably it was not the day for the Why-Walk. But, as promised, transport arrived in the shape of Mr Humphreys's hill-climbing grocery van. Orders Promptly Delivered Whatever the Distance.

My weekly box of iron rations was carried in by Mr H – 'Terrible cough today. Mind you don't spread it on the wireless!' – and within half an hour I was myself promptly delivered back to the high street shop. Fortified by a fresh ham roll from Mrs Humphreys, I could pick up a taxi here, as long as there wasn't a funeral on. Mr Pritchard, of Majestic Motors Maes-y-Melyn, ran a system of strict priority as far as his black Daimler was concerned. But with luck I might make Ruabon station, ten miles further on, in time for the Shrewsbury connection to Wolverhampton, and so onto the last lap of the day to Euston.

Once aboard there might even be time to study the programme scripts delivered by Dewi the Post just yesterday. Crumpled into a carrier bag they had almost been left behind under the trays of farmhouse cobs and large Hovis going out next on Mr Humphreys's round.

Usually, though, it was hard to concentrate. From my seat by the window, I was too caught up in the melancholy sight of a receding Wales as we rattled towards the border. Hills and valleys fell away into the mist. Telford's fantastical viaduct rose up over the river, like some gateway to Arcadia, before that too disappeared into the past. There was a glimpse down a lane of the last sign-post saying Croeso i Cymru, Welcome to Wales. Once again I saw the invisible line of my childhood snaking across the landscape, dividing home ground from that other country where I did not belong.

As we travelled on, changing voices around me marked the transition. The lively rise and fall of the Welsh gave way to Shropshire burrs which fast became overlaid by the metallic flatness of the Midlands and the South-East. Then, all too soon, we were at Euston and I was swallowed up by hordes of hurrying robots. I thought of Will's reaction to the crowds, the only time he had been to London – 'and all breathing the same breath too!'

The wafts of polluted air, the bellowing announcements, the glare and confusion of the concourse always took me aback. It was only a forerunner of what lay ahead, I would remind myself. How had the big city which I knew so well become alien territory with an impact that was almost threatening? I knew the answer, of course. I had sold my soul to Hafod, a Faustian pact which would no doubt demand its payments from me in one way or another.

Within a week or two, of course, I would adjust, on the surface at least. New experiences soon diverted me from the wrench of parting from Wales. Strangely enough, it was that interview with the King that helped to bridge the gap on the very next day. We had first met ten years before in his Victorian seaside palace after the splendours of his coronation. A few years later there was a dawn encounter at the island's famous Stonehenge when His Majesty demonstrated that this monument, like its English counterpart, was a primitive marker for the summer solstice. Such things seemed to happen in Tonga.

Now here we were in London, both of us admitting to missing home, the mighty Taufa'ahau Tupou IV ensconced on a very large sofa at the High Commission residence, me on a slightly lower level opposite, shoes removed Polynesian-style, while we discussed with some animation the curious rapport between Tonga and Wales. Rugby, and male voice choirs, Methodist Sundays, the impact of foreign tourists on language and culture were the main topics of conversation as a happy hour went by. Finally the ceremonial *kava* was served. My intrigued producer, Annie Howells, put away the microphone and expressed herself well pleased with the recording. As I left,

His Majesty presented me with a large envelope, stamped with his personal seal.

'Just a few corrections,' he murmured. Apparently my publishers had sent the royal expert a proof copy of my new book, the one I finished that first week at Hafod. 'It is a very interesting book,' he added consolingly, in that soft voice of his. 'But I know what sticklers we authors are when it comes to spelling.'

'Now I know why you loved the Pacific,' Annie remarked, as we drove back to Broadcasting House. 'Do you still miss it?'

'Not now I have Wales,' I said.

'And when you're in London what do you miss about Wales?' asked Annie.

I thought for a minute. 'The things that make me feel Welsh: the talk, curiosity about other people, smiles in the shops, my mountain, of course, even the weather. You don't get weather in London, only temperatures.'

Annie said she wished the English would take us more seriously for she herself came from Carmarthenshire. All those knee-jerk reactions . . .

'Taffy was a Welshman, Taffy was a thief . . . '

'Witches' hats and slag-heaps.'

'Dylan Thomas being a drunken fraud.'

'The joke accents – the "look-you" and the "indeed-to-goodness"!'

Perhaps we had a chip on our shoulders, one of us said, which made us laugh. It wouldn't be surprising, though, the way the English had been keeping us down ever since they started building those grim border castles.

'Talk about colonial rule.'

'Wait till independence, though. They say in North Wales there'll be a Welsh parliament before long, if Plaid Cymru have anything to do with it.'

We were back at Broadcasting House. Out of habit we lowered our voices. No one gossips in a BBC lift. Usually no one speaks. Men with beards clasped their clipboards to them like breastplates and looked thoughtfully down at their brown suede shoes. Back in the *Woman's Hour* corridor, there was, at least, a highly-strung kind of camaraderie. Broadcasting live on a daily programme boosted the adrenalin levels alarmingly although, as presenter, I tried not to get too carried away. So many pitfalls lurked unseen. There was the rather stately lunch beforehand when the VIP guest was supposed to relax among equally nervous fellow contributors. In the background a gaggle of producers would still be debating in fraught undertones the exact order of play. As for me, I was doing my best to get a word in edgeways with my interviewee-to-be. There was always a last minute hiatus. Kingsley Amis demanded a second whisky and Jonathan Miller lost his glasses. Germaine Greer needed the loo. Lady Longford was looking for the back of an envelope where she'd scribbled her extra notes about the Duke of Wellington. There was also the well-known actor who liked to have a standard lamp to read by and another who always brought a favourite cushion. In the studio, once round the baize table – so handy for sweaty palms – I had an idiosyncrasy of my own. This was my determination to avoid wearing headphones. Without all those well-meaning instructions from the control room, I felt totally free to concentrate on whoever I was talking to, free also from the tinny echo of my own voice inside my head. So instead, I became expert at 'going on the green', that is, jumping in on cue the instant the green light flashed in front of me.

'Bloody Welsh always have to be different,' said the sound engineer with a wink. But it seemed to work and, I suppose, by temperament, I liked to be independent. As it was, with the afternoon slot there was always the extra hassle of fitting in the two o'clock pips and the news headlines, usually just as the guest interview was getting into its stride. Through the glass I would catch a glimpse of an excitable producer, waving her arms with fury or approval, as the case might be. Then, when the serial arrived, a blessed lull would descend, except for the time Dame Edna Everage was still in the studio with me, completely wrecking my introduction to 'the story so far'. Theme music was faded up fast to cover the collapse of the presenter. Nevertheless many listeners must have found it difficult to adjust to the romantic atmosphere of that particular serial in the wake of Dame Edna's version of the plotline.

Love *Woman's Hour* as I did, the making of features and documentary programmes was the kind of broadcasting I most enjoyed. In *One Woman's Arabia*, a flash-back to my five years in the Yemen and my *Double Life* series on biographers, for instance, and the story of the Victorian diarist, Francis Kilvert, there was time to interview in depth and write a fully fledged script. Every now and then I also had to take over *Pick of the Week* which gave me new insights into what the best kind of radio could do.

Coming home each evening, it was often hard to assimilate all those crowded impressions, hard to find a space of my own inside my head. Back at the flat R was wrestling with the problems of various controversial court cases. Fortunately for both of us, our tiny top-floor abode had certain Hafod-like qualities which helped to banish stress.

'Why do you always live in the clouds?' our friends would ask plaintively as they toiled up the five flights to our attic in Park Street. Mayfair is an imposing address but the reality was rather different. It was a fine old house, too thin for a lift, and refurbishments did not extend to what had once been the quarters of a long-vanished troupe of servants, no doubt some of them Welsh runaways like ourselves.

We felt at home there right from the start. The ceilings were low and, as at the cottage, walls and floors were on a friendly slant. No picture hung straight and every rug crept furtively sideways to the nearest door. Gaping floorboards sometimes yielded buried treasure, a battered tin snuff-box, a Victorian hook for fastening boot-buttons in haste, as an impatient summons came from below.

Hurrying down was easy when you came to the main staircase which was wide and curved. Behind our door, however, the top flight of stairs was more like a ladder, narrow and steep, as befitted the comings and goings of the lower orders. Overhead was a glass cupola and through it the full moon would look down at us with a smug Mayfair smile. I found it hard to believe that this was the same Hafod moon, no doubt scudding along at this very moment between the mountain tops and the owl-haunted valleys.

Here in London, 'Home for Christmas' was the watchword, a familiar mantra which had a new pull to it now there was Hafod waiting for us at the other end. Christmas in Wales had an even more powerful resonance somehow. Dylan Thomas had seen to that with his glorious recreation of a child's-eye view of the 'bright white snowball of Christmas'. Only a few days before, I was interviewing the actor Emlyn Williams about his autobiography and he had conjured up a fond memory of a Christmas treat which I shared, coming from the same part of Wales. The panto matinée at the Royalty Theatre, Chester, cast a never-to-be-forgotten spell over small-town children like us. Who could not thrill to the sounds of the orchestra tuning up (which Emlyn mistook for the miaowing of Dick Whittington's cat backstage), the glittering costumes as the curtain went up, the rows of mesmerized eyes pinpointed in the dark of the auditorium?

Anyone who has ever written about life in Wales seems to have included a Christmas scene. Usually there was a goose being plucked round a glowing range, the feathers to be stuffed into pillows, the goose-grease kept for bad chests. A white-haired grandfather, who looked like Lloyd George, would be declaiming grace at the head of the laden table with the fervour of an election manifesto. The Christmas Eisteddfod at the chapel also figured large with a shilling prize for the best young reciter of the fourteenth-century poet, Dafydd ap Gwilym.

Hafod too had begun to establish its own rituals. On our very first Christmas, mufflered carol-singers from the village climbed up to serenade us by lantern-light. The holly and the ivy came from our own trees and there were sledge rides down the icy helter-skelter of the track.

Why is it then that the moments of disaster are the ones that stand out most indelibly? Remember Mr Protheroe, for instance. This was the time when a heavier than usual avalanche of soot meant a Christmas Eve visit from a sweep if we were to have the yule logs blazing the next day. This being Wales, Mr Protheroe was no ordinary sweep. A bald, stumpy man, long retired from the merchant navy, he relived most of the highlights of his foreign travels during the six hours spent investigating our various fireplaces and assorted chimneys. Halfway through, the whisky decanter was sighted. Toasts were raised to the navies of the world. ('The Turks were the ones to look out for – not many people know that!') Brushes and bellows and huge canvas bags were trundled on a trolley from one room to the next. A fine black dust settled on the tinsel chains and freezing blasts blew in from the ever-open doors. ('Cold's nothing to me – I've been on the Russia run, remember!')

In a prolonged farewell, Mr Protheroe declared that Wales couldn't hold him forever. He was getting itchy feet again.

'But Protheroe, Post Restante, Shanghai, will always find me,' he promised as he lurched away on his ancient motorbike and sidecar, trailing a plume of sooty smoke in his wake.

First thing Christmas morning another avalanche descended. There was a unanimous decision to retreat to family in Wrexham for the day.

The Christmas before the car was the casualty. After a late-night party it had taken it into its head to slip off the brakes and go for a run on its own. In the cold light of dawn the wandering machine was found lying peacefully on its side at the bottom of the mountain. 'Did you have a good party, then?' was Will's way of reporting his discovery on the phone, long before the rest of us were up. That was the first but not the last time the Lada was rescued by Dai Breakdown, a one-man emergency service more often referred to, not surprisingly, as Dai Nervous Breakdown.

Compared with these episodes, most problems were trivial – the dead mouse at the bottom of the sloe gin, the giant turkey that, despite drastic surgical amputations, still spurned our oven and had to be cooked next day at the farm.

A dull rainy Christmas was perhaps the worst disappointment of all. Frost was better. But so far we had never had snow. In London, the television forecast seemed hopeful this year if the weather map of the British Isles was anything to go by. Snow symbols covered the green Wales-shaped protuberance on the left almost as thickly as those electronic blizzards that filled our screen at Hafod, thanks to 'poor local reception'. (Sammy Sparks's problems with a cable that ran through the Pen-y-Bryn cowshed didn't help either.)

In the maelstrom of Oxford Street only Bing Crosby and Nat King Cole seemed concerned with the idea of a white Christmas. Deafened by amplified music, battered by a thousand shopping bags and the sight of so many harassed faces, I was glad to escape onto the train at Euston. I fell asleep and woke again at Shrewsbury. In the dusk, as promised, the first flakes were falling over the Welsh hills. The lady from Ruthin sitting opposite me nodded sagely.

'*Eira mawr, eira man.* That's what they always say.'

Big snow, little snow was her translation, meaning that the large loose flakes always melted fast, even as they touched the ground.

For a moment, I felt absurdly disappointed. In my mind was a fixed image of a Christmas card Hafod, time and change blotted out under that goose-down white, with just a smoking chimney or two down at the farms, a light in a cottage window, a stranded mail-coach up on the Pass. I knew quite well that the reality of being cut off by snow had nothing to do with any of this. It had happened to us before, but never at Christmas. Even so, just this once . . .

Anyway, Welsh proverbs were notoriously inaccurate, I told myself, as the train drew in at Ruabon station. Ruabon was Wales. I was home again and under the light at the end of the platform was the snow-speckled figure of R, waiting to meet me.

13

WIZARD PASSIONS

'Griff's been up doing some repairs,' said R, who had come up a few days earlier with the usual carload of presents and provisions. Griff was a newcomer to Hafod, a stocky Hercules proverbially capable of 'turning his hand to anything'. He had first arrived to off-load an avalanche of logs from his tractor, clear all the roof gutters, raze a vertical acre of wilderness, and stoke up the biggest bonfire ever seen on our side of the mountain. There was no mention of work on the house. But Griff was a law to himself, as everyone reminded me.

'What sort of repairs?' I asked nervously, while we trundled along into Llangollen.

'Can't remember exactly,' R replied.

He was concentrating on avoiding the town fire-engine which was coming towards us at speed, all bells ringing. Instantly Griff's bonfires sprang to mind. Was this to be the Christmas disaster to beat all others? But it was only Santa (Chief Fire Officer Haydon Hughes) perched on top of his scarlet chariot in full beard and robes, making his rounds of the children's parties.

Other Llangollen rituals were in full swing. Around the town hall Christmas tree the Fron Silver Band was pumping out 'Shepherds Watched' while the Hebron Mixed Choir carried on in rich counterpoint from the chapel steps with the *Messiah*. 'Every valley shall be exalted,' the ladies warbled to the surrounding hills. 'And the rough places plain,' boomed the tenors and the basses, heads thrown back while the snow drifted down from the crags of Dinas Brân Castle . . . I had forgotten how in Wales people could be transformed by this passion for singing, voices surging, faces alight. Fresh to it again, I stood entranced.

But I had shopping to collect. Inside Ellis Greengrocers they were doing a brisk trade in chestnuts and tangerines.

'Snow for Christmas,' announced little Mrs Ellis.

This was my cue. '*Eira mawr, eira man,*' I replied knowledgeably from among the Brussels sprouts.

There was a startled silence. 'Sorry?'

Mr Ellis came to my rescue. 'Picking it up then, are you? Very good! *Da iawn.*'

'Well, she is Welsh, after all, isn't she?' said the lady next to me, with an encouraging dig in the ribs. '*Chwarae teg.* Fair play.'

'*Chwarae teg,*' I agreed.

Lest more should be required I turned to the holly.

Wreaths could still be ordered, Mrs E reminded me. 'For the cemetery, that is. We don't hang them on our doors in Wales, do we? Looks morbid somehow.'

Paper chains and balloons were more the style over at the butchers where the turkey was faithfully promised for the next day.

'Not too big this time, is it?' they chaffed. Across the road at Lewis-Jones Drapers and Chemists, a splendid window display was drawing admirers, as befitted a famous establishment founded 'When Victoria Was Queen'. Family Antiques provided a cosy setting. An oak dresser hung with Welsh tweed loomed large. Hand-knitted shawls and sheepskin jackets nestled around a gold Eisteddfod harp. But the *pièce de résistance* was a Victorian sledge piled with 'ideal gifts' and tastefully embedded in a drift of cotton wool from the pharmacy next door. This was apparently the brainchild of the stately Mrs L-J herself.

'I rode on that when I was a child,' she told me. This was upstairs where she was enthroned in a kind of iron cage presiding over the wire-and-pulley cash transactions. 'I'm only here part-time these days,' she confided. 'Now I'm eighty-nine I need a bit of relaxation, they tell me.'

Further down at the newsagents the festive spirit was running wild. Old Mr Parry was especially proud of his papier mâché Welsh dragon, framed with fairy lights and brandishing a druidical spray of mistletoe in its jaws. Next door Tick-Tock Price who repaired clocks had stolen a march by looking ahead. A picture of Old Father Time bore the slogan, 'Greet the New Year with one of our new Battery-Operated Alarm Clocks. £5.50 Special Reduction.'

'Typical Tick-Tock,' I heard from a passer-by. 'Always on the make, even at Christmas time.'

I recognized the sharp tones of our local historian, a small bent figure in a purple cape. Miss Parry-Williams and I had not exchanged many greetings since our encounter at Benny's saleroom in pursuit of Dr Johnson's *Dictionary*. In haste as usual, she was weighed down by a large basket of papers and pamphlets, one of which she thrust into my bag.

'Clwyd Historical Society New Year Lecture. "Dialect Studies of the Welsh in Patagonia". Better be there!'

Pushing her bicycle before her, she hurried on. 'Late as usual,' she snapped to herself, rather like Alice's Rabbit.

'Wouldn't it be quicker to get on it?' I suggested.

'Haven't got time,' she called back, no doubt on her way to the Mad Hatter's Tea Party.

After all this bustle, it was a relief to get to Hafod. By now there was a thin powdering of snow over the mountain. As usual all the lights were on from end to end of the house. I was like Robert Louis Stevenson who always had the lamps burning late at Vailima so that he could see the glow of the windows through the trees as he rode up to his 'beautiful, shining, windy house'. Christmas it might be but there was no sign of any shepherds watching their flocks up there. No doubt both Will and Owen would be making their usual torch-light rounds of the fields later, on the look-out for wily foxes who had their holes in the Eglwyseg rocks. Around midnight Will often hung lanterns in the trees to keep them away. But the lure of young lambs, the heads especially, was too strong for them. Ten had been taken in just one month on Gwen's farm alone.

Inside the house, the presence of Gwen was evident as always, with fresh clearings made for the progress of the hoover through the ever-encroaching jungle of books and papers.

Usually a bulletin was left on the table reporting bat droppings in the spare bedroom, or the urgent need for a new mop. This time there was a WI calendar instead and a box of mince pies.

There was a note propped up, half-hidden among the piles of cards and shiny paper but it was not from Gwen.

Printed in large letters the message was mysterious, ominous even. 'WINDOWS BRICKED UP O.K. HAPPY XMAS GRIFF.'

What windows, for Heaven's sake? And why? For a moment my blood ran cold. At the BBC I had just been recording a programme about Borley Rectory, the most haunted house in England, where they'd had to block up the dining-room window to discourage the phantom nun from peering in from the shrubbery. At Hafod, perhaps, it was the Valle Crucis monks who'd been causing trouble.

'Only the coal-house,' R said soothingly.

Of course. We'd decided some time ago that the broken panes in the back served no purpose at all except to let in the rain and, at this moment, the snow. Sure enough, we found out that an assortment of old Ruabon bricks had been plastered together to replace the glass. Much cheered, we returned inside to take stock of preparations. Howard and

Vanessa were out with friends. But they had brought in a small, withered-looking fir tree that now sat crouched in a fire-bucket in a corner of the parlour. It was adorned with home-made decorations that showed the wear and tear of our travelling years but were still dear to us. Sprigs of our own holly and ivy had been tucked artistically behind every picture and Griff's birch and sycamore logs burned with a sweet resinous scent in the usually temperamental fireplaces. Not a speck of soot was to be seen. The dining-room walls were now the deep yellow colour recommended by Megan as being discouraging to flies. In the parlour Gwen's rose-patterned wallpaper had repaid the stripping of ten different layers beneath, ending in Victorian blue distemper. In the lamplight glow we made our shopping lists for tomorrow and told ourselves we were 'just in time' before the weather took hold.

'Just in time' became the password of the next two days. As a precaution we left the car down by the stream, and carried our last provisions up the track, with the turkey triumphantly impaled on Owen's pitchfork like the eagle on a Roman standard.

'Watch out, though. Could well be freezing tonight!'

Sure enough, on Christmas morning, the thin snow had turned to marble.

'Socks over boots. Gives a grip, see,' Megan instructed as we slithered to a halt at the farm. They had to be the right sort of socks though, those home-knitted affairs with the knobbly consistency of yesterday's porridge. Luckily, they seemed to be in plentiful supply at Pen-y-Bryn. So were the sacks of brown salt for gritting the lane, turning the icy surface into a rich Christmas cake mixture.

Between the socks and the salt, the four of us got to the car and so to church. This was morning service at the little St Tysilio's in the next valley, tucked away for five centuries with the mountain at its back, the river at its feet. The place was packed and the Reverend Maldwyn Jones had his work cut out to get the congregation served in good order at the Communion rail. A short, bearded man, bursting with South Wales enthusiasm, he was on this occasion assisted by a sombre-looking cleric from Caernarfonshire. The visitor was advanced in years and somewhat shaky in his movements. Even so, nothing quite prepared us for the moment when the last wafer slipped from his fingers and disappeared between his boots.

'Bloody Hell!' he exploded under his breath.

It was clear enough for the row of faces on either side to freeze visibly in the effort not to laugh. A suppressed snuffle ran round the choir, red-cheeked farm children in their matching red caps and gowns. From behind his green baize curtain, old Mr Pugh, the organist, broke into a tremulous version of 'Sheep May Safely Graze' while Maldwyn helped him regain his composure with the aid of the last few drops of Communion wine.

Meanwhile the sun had come out, streaming through the brilliantly coloured east window in the style of Burne-Jones, and nearby, in a fragment of fifteenth-century stained glass, the figure of St James, patron of pilgrims. Back in our seats there was time to absorb this heady mix of the medieval and the Victorian. A familiar whiff of candle-wax and Brasso and fresh-cut greenery hung in the air, more potent than any incense. As always, for me it was the poet Browning who dominated the place. Late in life, years after the death of Elizabeth, he was a regular guest at the nearby house of the local magnate, Sir Theodore Martin. Attending service with the family, the great man was always asked to read the lesson. Even now that leonine head and resonant voice still seemed to hover over the great oak-eagle lectern. I imagined the melancholy widower wandering afterwards among the gravestones outside, where the fields sloped down to the falls and sheep had safely grazed for as long as anyone could remember. No Pre-Raphaelite painter could have asked for more.

Inside the church, though, it was Lady Martin I liked to remember. As Helena Faucit she was the most famous

Shakespearean actress of her day, a special favourite of Browning's. There she was this Christmas morning at the end of our usual pew, outlined in graceful profile on the memorial stone in her name. Her husband, too, was an esteemed figure in Victorian London, lawyer, writer and entrepreneur. But together they loved to escape from society to the wilds of North Wales.

Not everything went smoothly in their romantic endeavours to turn an old cottage into an Italianate country house. Not long ago I came across her diaries which spoke to me like a voice in my ear. 'Wants without number,' she wrote. 'These workmen fill me with despair.' Touching a particular chord came the entry, 'Oh, so cold! Snow on the hills this morning and hailstones through the day. This little nest has too many draughts for rough weather.'

Slowly though, Helena transformed Bryntysilio into the perfect retreat of her imagination. Browning always treasured his visits there, remembering 'those sweet starry Sundays at the little church leading to the House Beautiful'. Delighted with Sir Theodore's biography of the late Prince Albert, Queen Victoria also came to inspect this heaven on earth, taking tea on the lawn while the massed voices of the Llangollen choir added to the charm of the occasion.

Helena died in October 1898. 'When the end came,' her husband wrote, 'it was in our quiet Welsh home where she had been able to look out upon the garden she loved and the circling amphitheatre of many shadowed hills that had been her delight for years.'

At first I used to assume that the small medallion portrait at the bottom corner of the memorial was Sir Theodore himself. Tucked away beneath the actress's flowing skirts like an obedient spaniel, it always seemed to me an undignified position for her husband. But, of course, the bearded profile was none other than Shakespeare's, as I reminded myself, looking more closely. Meanwhile Maldwyn was coming to the end of his Christmas homily. Lost in the past, I was sorry to have missed it. His sermons often created quite a stir. Only a year ago he had mounted the pulpit carrying a shot-gun. This was to point up his theme which was the absurdity of armed force by civilized nations in this day and age. Surely Wales, at least, should remain aloof from such folly.

Driving home we found that a rise in the temperature had loosened the grip of the frost. The lane to Hafod was passable for cars, briefly anyway.

'Just in time,' everyone said, once again, as family visitors converged to make some inroads on the turkey (cooked the night before with power cuts in mind), also the pudding and Christmas cake and other extras by courtesy of Humphreys Grocery and the Cottage Bakery. As friends of various ages appeared and disappeared Hafod itself seemed to expand in spirit. Perhaps the house was remembering the rough-and-tumble Christmases of a hundred years ago, spartan as they must have been for the labouring families of those days. According to the Parochial List of Indoor and Outdoor Poor, the widow, Jane Jones, had been fortunate to receive £1 and 2 shillings for the half-year. There would be plenty of wood to burn though, a pig killed for feasting and keeping, kind neighbours, and perhaps some precious oranges in silver paper from the Llangollen market.

'The snow! Look, the snow!' the children would have cried when it eventually arrived, as we did. Looking out on Boxing Day there was that transformation which is always a miracle. No one had seen it actually fall which made it all the more magical, like some celestial sleight-of-hand. All through the night it must have come down, so that by morning Hafod was wrapped in a gigantic muff of snow. The sun was glittering in a blue sky and the familiar landscape had turned itself into that archetypal Christmas card. No one had written on it yet. This whiteness had been left blank for messages.

As far as the eye could see, paths and lanes, the mountain slopes and the farm below were all in disguise, every surface smoothly masked. Outside the gate the Lada was an igloo and away up on the Pass there was a small Eskimo village of stranded cars. The silence everywhere was so intense it was like suddenly going deaf. No phone rang. The burden of snow had proved too much for our spider's web of communication lines, the electricals included.

I feel a secret delight at first in this sense of a Hafod even more cut off than usual. But survival tactics take over, especially as the sun has gone in and the air is veiled with the threat of more snow to come. First there is a path to be dug up to the little pony-shed where Rosie is lying in state, the smug centrepiece of her own nativity scene. Four minute and bleary offspring are bunched up around her in the straw. Vanessa and her friends had spent most of yesterday evening attending her accouchement which, being her second, was mercifully trouble-free.

In the house there is no shortage of food. Fires are lit and urgent cries go up.

'Where do we keep the candles?'

'Where's the old kettle?'

'Any oil for the lamps?'

Naturally Gwen has foreseen just this situation. The lamps are already filled. Three stone hot-water bottles, circa 1900, have been retrieved from some hiding-place. Spare buckets have been placed at the ready near pipes that might soon be fit to burst. There's even a tub of cinders left by the back door, the traditional dressing for frozen paths.

Other members of the community are making their own arrangements. A small stoat, brown on top, winter white beneath, has discovered that the best way of retrieving the turkey carcass from the bird-table is by biting through the string and rolling it down the bank into the cover of the rhododendron bushes. Our woodpecker, black and white with a flash of scarlet, is up the telegraph pole drilling for buried insects. Away in the furthest field I can see Will and the boys taking feed to the sheep, tiny Brueghel figures, black against the snow. Voices ring out faintly to and fro like battle-cries. An arm is raised towards Hafod.

'All right up there, are you?'

'Yes, all right so far!'

Later on, from down by the brook came the hornet's buzz of the chainsaw as they took turns to cut extra wood. More snow fell, a blizzard this time, gusting sideways up the valley towards the north so that the whole landscape became a blur. Even in the shelter of our mountain, the drifts piled up and it was three days before the post got through.

'Climbed up from the other side, I did,' said Dewi. 'Couldn't get the van any further than the lane.'

He had collapsed in the kitchen, legs stuck out like a pair of plaster casts. Now he was steaming gently over a mug of tea, defrosting his moustache with a large red handkerchief.

Feeling guilty that the mail was mostly late Christmas cards, I made fresh tea and plied him for news. Dewi allowed himself a pause.

'Heard about the Beast, I expect?' he asked casually.

'The Beast?'

There was another pause, building the suspense.

'Saw the footprints myself, just yesterday first thing. Going up under the Forestry, they were, not far from Pant Glas. Other people have seen them too, when the snow first came down.'

'What sort of footprints?' was the next obvious question.

'Sort of round pads. With claw-marks in front. Funny thing was they were all in a straight line, one in front of the other.' Dewi's hands came down flat on the table to demonstrate.

It was a thrilling moment. I found myself thinking of Megan's Field of the She-Bear. Could there even now be one last descendant lurking in the forest above? More practically, perhaps it was a large polecat, a vanishing species still to be found in Wales. I'd never seen its footprints. But on one of our 'digs' into old cottage rubbish-pits, we had both caught sight of a furry grey shape with a long tail slipping down through the fir trees on the track to Valle Crucis. I remembered something else too, how Will had once told me about finding a dead lamb with a hole in its throat where the blood had been sucked away – 'A terrible smell too, sure sign of a polecat.'

Even this gory tale was too tame for Dewi.

'No, no. Some kind of monster it is, like one of those Yeti they found up in the Himalayas. Somewhere like Wales, anyway.'

Briskly he downed his tea and buttoned up his jacket again. Some of the elderly people higher up the valley were marooned in their cottages. So he was in demand and not just for the mail either. Only yesterday he'd chopped some morning sticks to get a fire going for one of them and dug a path to the *ty bach* for an old lady with a frozen WC.

'And back in town there's Mrs Thomas's pension to be collected. Oh, and old Hywel's water to be taken in.'

He saw me looking puzzled.

'Specimen for the Doc. Got the bladder-trouble bad again, hasn't he? No wonder with this weather.'

Whistling, he set off down the bank, bag over his shoulder.

'Mind, look out for the old Yeti on Saturday,' he called back to Howard.

Boxing Day is the traditional day for the farmers' fox-shoot. But this year it had been postponed and the snow had almost cleared when Howard set out with Aled and about thirty others on the annual expedition to bring the killers to justice. Back home that evening he reported a respectable total of six executions, which was good news for the beleaguered shepherds and chicken farmers. An enthusiastic assortment of 'hounds' in the shape of the local collies, had worked well flushing the foxes out of the rocks. But it had been a hard slog on foot and by Land Rover up and down the surrounding mountainsides.

'The best thing were the stops,' Howard said dreamily, as his sister pulled off his boots for him.

Being a gentle soul by nature it was the glorious succession of farmhouse refreshments that remained the most memorable part of the day as far as he was concerned.

'Now it's your turn to go on safari,' I was told next morning.

Something called a Solstice Climb had been planned for some time, a heroic-sounding expedition to find a certain stone circle on top of the Eglwyseg moors. There we were to commune with our Bronze Age ancestors, sustained by a hearty picnic and the famous Panorama view of the surrounding country.

'But the solstice has gone,' I protested. 'December the twenty-first, remember.'

'Never mind. It's to celebrate the New Year instead,' said Vanessa firmly.

Tomorrow they would be gone to spend the rest of the holiday with friends. So, leaving R behind with his new Wodehouse anthology and Rosie with her pups, the three of us set off towards the looming limestone escarpment of the Eglwyseg. Soon we found ourselves in the narrow lane running along the foot of it. Howard inspected the map, looking for a short cut up. I was all for short cuts, especially as what the guide-book described as a 'mild scramble' now appeared to be a crash course in mountaineering.

But Howard had already disappeared up a gap in the rock-face hidden in the undergrowth.

'This is the gully, all right,' said the voice above me. 'There's a bit of a stream but it's the easiest way, like the book says.'

Vanessa was reassuringly close behind me. Even so, it was a mistake to look down. There was a vertiginous glimpse of the lane far below. A thorn tree had entangled itself in my hair. My unsuitable wellingtons produced an ominous slithering sensation just as a loose stone came bounding past.

'Think I'll go back,' I heard myself announce, coming to a standstill.

This was, of course, impossible. Helpful hands and firm exhortations got me going again until we reached an old sheep-track halfway up.

'You can see the top now,' came the cheerful cry ahead.

In fact, as I was to discover, there is no such thing as the top in this part of the world. Once we were over the first brow, another appeared, and then another. But at least there was flat turf to sit on and time to bring out sandwiches and a flask of tea from the crumpled carrier-bag a true climber would have scorned.

Now there was nothing but empty scrubland rolling away on either side, with shreds of fox-coloured bracken here and there and a few last patches of snow. There was no sign of the Panorama path, no sign of any standing stones, either. The promised views of valleys and villages seemed to have disappeared into another dimension. It was three in the afternoon and the light was already beginning to die a little. A wind had got up, whipping across the bleak horizon out of nowhere.

Something strange happened to me up here. It was no longer a fear of heights that came over me but the idea of never finding the way back.

'Let's search for the circle another time,' I suggested cravenly. 'Hadn't we better start looking for a way down?'

But Howard was walking on, Vanessa behind him. 'Can't be far from here,' he called back.

I tried not to think of all the stories of people getting lost on these moors, falling down old mine-shafts, wandering off the track in bad weather. But there was something else too. I hadn't so far set eyes on any sign of prehistoric times. Yet in all that emptiness there was a sense of occupation. Long ago others had made this place their own, somewhere to keep a look-out for the enemy, to examine the skies and give back the dead to the all-demanding gods. The thought that we were not welcome here came into my mind. You could not call it panic exactly, rather a strong sense of threat. But standing alone for a moment, I had never wanted to leave a place so much, as the silence settled around me and the shadows gathered.

I knew I had felt like this somewhere before, somewhere far away. Then I remembered Kiribati, the loneliest of Pacific atolls, finding myself on what Robert Louis Stevenson called 'the accursed ocean shore, fit scene for wizardry and shipwreck'. This was the deserted side of the island, open to the wildest of weather, a place still scattered with fragments of the sacred platforms where prayers and sacrifices were made by the priests to the invisible rulers of life and death. Now, as then, I had that same sense of being an intruder. More than that, though, I was an eavesdropper on ceremonies that had left behind them some hint of ancient danger, a forgotten power that could imprison you in a different time, perhaps forever.

A voice of the here and now called out from over the nearest rise. Vanessa had found what looked like traces of one of the settlements. It was only a flattened hollow in the ground, layered down to about three feet and surrounded by small boulders, scarred and pitted with age. Together we stood in the small depression in the centre that looked like a hearth. Mysteriously the sense of threat vanished. This was a place of family, of women and children especially, a retreat from danger. Trying to imagine it was like looking at a tiny picture at the far end of an immense telescope, four thousand years long.

I wished I had Will's bronze axe-head with me. Found in the fields below, it was such a little thing, so smooth and delicately made with a finish like green marble, it seemed more like a domestic tool than a killing weapon. In the palm of my hand it would have felt like a talisman, a charm of some kind, to conjure up those long-gone spirits of the place.

Far away to the west the great fortress shape of the limestone range was caught in a fan-shaped burst of light.

The invisible sun was going down behind the clouds. With luck we might still be able to see the way down.

At the same moment, over the horizon came the figure of Howard. In triumph he told us how he had found some standing stones, about forty of them in a rough circle about twenty yards across. But there was neither time nor tape-measure to examine them properly.

Next time, we all said, perhaps on the summer solstice, or a midsummer's eve. But now we were caught in the bleak mid-winter, at the end of one of the shortest days, looking for any other sign of life that might appear. Who else, though, would be crazy enough to climb along the Eglwyseg at twilight, at this time of the year?

Sheep, was the answer. Sure enough, round a clump of stunted trees, a ghostly procession of them appeared, eyes phosphorescent in the half-light. Gratefully we followed them down the track. Further along, the sight of an old gate was as reassuring as a sign-post. We had come safely to the bottom edge of the escarpment. In the distance we could see the outline of Dinas Brân Castle and beneath it the silvery coil of the Dee and the lights of Llangollen. As we walked on there was the comforting clang of milk-churns from the nearest farm, dogs barking, familiar farmyard smells. And past the farm there finally appeared the faint glimmer of the lane that marked the line of Offa's Dyke and the way home to Hafod . . .

My dreams that night had a troubling quality, though. The presence of the past up by the stones was formidable and lived on in my mind. The Eglwyseg was not the kind of place I would like to wander without company, I told myself, even on a fine day.

As usual, the young Coleridge had a good phrase for the uneasy dreamer, something about starting from precipices of distempered sleep. On his scrambles among the mountains of North Wales in the year of that poem, perhaps he too had been lured on by the precipices of Eglwyseg. Tonight, at any rate, the strange hallucinatory images seemed to take on a new meaning. Those moonlight roundelays now belonged to the circle of standing stones. And in that forsaken place, as I well knew, the Wizard Passions were still weaving 'an holy spell' . . .

14

CONSULTING DOCTOR IVOR

All Welsh mountains deserve to be treated with respect. In the eighteenth century, visitors from England reeled back from them in some dismay, grasping at adjectives such as 'monstrous', 'aweful' and 'barbarous' in their efforts to describe these forbidding frontiers of an alien land.

Our own small mountain is an altogether different affair. Its very name, Fron Fawr (meaning great hill, or great bosom, according to context), reflects its rolling, rounded contours, mother earth rather than tribal fortress. In summer its slopes are green and thick with fern, criss-crossed by sheep paths and some wind-blown fencing where Will and his predecessors laid their boundaries, right up to the top. Somewhere along here is the spot where Will struck his foot on the little bronze axe-head, as he dug in one of the posts. Further across, above the old barn, is the hidden spring that is now our well. Before pipes were laid children from nearby would carry water home from here. Farm carts went up the old drovers' track to collect the dry bracken for bedding, animal and human, until quite recent times.

So, as you walk, there is always a sense of other people, past and present, on Fron Fawr. In its shadow runs the path to the abbey and the crossing over the brook that leads through the fields to the Llangollen road. Halfway up there's a long-disused rifle range and an old notice-board still nailed up to warn you of 'DANGER when the flag is flying'. The scattered crofts and cottages are mostly gone, but certain names on the early survey maps give clues in tiny smudged italics. The sheep like to make themselves comfortable against any remaining stones which have rooted themselves in the moss. And not far away there's always a fragment or two of blue-and-white china to be found, a chip of green bottle-glass or the rusty heel of an old boot resurrected from the household rubbish pit somewhere below the surface.

I used to wonder who had actually owned this mountain of ours in the first place, if anyone, or if it had always been common land, up for grabs to anyone who fancied it. Then, about this time, there came my way an evocative slip of paper which was part of a record of local land rentals, dated 1649. As a result, my picture of Fron Fawr's past was suddenly taken over by the dashing figure of one Sir Evan Lloyd who rejoiced in the romantic title of Knight of the Mountain Lands.

Because the paper is a photocopy of the original page, I can read the spiky black writing of the records clerk as if it were penned yesterday. The noble knight was apparently levied a sum of ten pounds per annum for his leasehold of two hundred acres. One of his tenants, 'the late wief of Rich ap Hugh', paid him five pounds per annum for her own holdings on the mountain. But now officialdom was demanding to know if Sir Evan was still in possession of his legal grant to the land.

The date explained this confrontation. It was the infamous year of the execution of Charles I. No doubt the zealous new agents of the Cromwellian regime had set their sights on the royalist knight. Hence the footnote to the entry:

'The said Sir Evan pleads to be in graunt but refuced to produce the same, saying *he would not trust us lest we should find any flawe in the same.*'

Here the report broke off. But I had the feeling that retribution would follow in the wake of such defiance. Strangely enough that sequel turned up without my even looking for it. A good friend with a splendid library produced 'an old book on Wales' for me to look at while we were staying at his house in Worcestershire. It was an eighteenth-century edition of Thomas Pennant's famous *Tours* of the country which recounted all kinds of tales of the past he'd picked up on his travels.

Handling it tenderly, I was somehow not surprised when the name of my swashbuckling hero sprang out of the page. It was a story that followed him into the 1650s, still a time of bitter enmity between the two factions, especially in the countryside.

In danger of his life, the Knight of the Mountain Lands took refuge in the house of a slippery local character known as *Cneifiwr Glas* or the Blue Fleecer, on account of his rapacity and the colour of his clothes. Although he was appointed a Land Steward by the 'usurpers', the Fleecer's speciality was to take in refugees from either side, depending on the size of the reward on offer.

Perhaps he had a soft spot for Sir Evan. Besides, he was a neighbour. At any rate, according to Pennant, with the fleeing royalist hidden in a cellar beneath the parlour floorboards, there followed a scene worthy of Shakespeare. Summoning the knight's pursuers, the Fleecer 'ordered them in a seeming rage to sally out in quest of Sir Evan. Stamping with his foot, he declared that if the knight was *above ground*, he would have him.'

Falling for the ruse, the Cromwellians dispersed to continue their hunt elsewhere. There is no mention of a capture so, one hopes, Sir Evan lived on to enjoy the Restoration. I like to think of him once more making his rounds of the Fron Fawr slopes that were so nearly snatched from him.

By the time Pennant was riding through, a hundred years later, the neighbourhood seems to have returned to its old undisturbed ways.

'This valley,' he wrote, 'is chiefly inhabited (happily) by an independent race of warm and wealthy yeomanry, undevoured as yet by the great men of the country.'

Independent, if not wealthy, was how my fellow-inhabitants seemed to me another two centuries on. Pennant had somehow caught the idyllic nature of 'the valley', still half-hidden from the rushing world beyond. A rose-coloured view, no doubt, now as then, I thought, as I clambered around the lower slopes of the mountain for my daily 'breath of fresh air'. An icy wind was blowing, whipping up the dead leaves in droves, the kind of weather to numb the bones of the field workers of the past and keep the poor of the parish indoors shivering over their gruel. Wind or not, I usually walk with my head down. Being an optimist, I always hope I might catch sight of another Bronze Age axe under my feet. This time though I was looking ahead. A strange marking on one of the oak trees caught my eye, curious enough to make me push through the undergrowth for a closer look. Startled, I found myself face to face with a large cross cut into the bark in the shape of a crucifix. It was obviously old, as the bare wood beneath was weathered and discoloured. Yet the outline still held firm, a curious sight in the middle of nowhere.

It was only then that I noticed the grave. At first I saw nothing more than a low grass-covered mound in a rocky hollow, just a few yards higher up. But there was a small stone at its head. In summer it would be covered by greenery, but now it was laid bare, firmly embedded in the ground. Just visible was some lettering.

I had to move closer and kneel down to read it. As I did so, I shivered. I heard in my head that old saying, 'someone just walked over my grave'. A name and a date was all the stone told me: 'Thomas Smithe 1801'. Whoever had made the inscription, rough as it was, had worked hard to chisel it deep enough to last. There was no room for more, perhaps no time. With so much left unsaid, one question followed another. Who was the unknown Thomas lying beneath? How had he died and why had he been buried so far from either church or village? There was also the mystery of the single date. Did it mean birth or death, and what was the connection with the cross?

Already the novelist in me was trying out some answers. This was unhallowed ground. Perhaps a suicide had been laid to rest here by his family, hidden away from local gossip. Or a dead baby, born out of wedlock, might have been given a name and secretly commemorated, despite the shame.

Crouched there by the grave, I felt guilty now, prying into a mystery that belonged to someone else. Whoever he was, time had swallowed him up along with all those other Fron Fawr presences – the neolithic settlers and the Valle Crucis monks, the royalist knight and the unnamed shepherds, woodcutters and cottagers. It was as if they had disappeared like the children of Hamelin into the enchanted mountain where, as in so many Celtic folktales, the unwary were lured away into a timeless underworld.

On the way home my mind was still working around that date on the stone. 1801 is historically close. I thought of the wars with the French, names like Napoleon, Nelson and mad King George. But did any of these relate to the remote Welsh countryside? Probably little enough. I needed to ask some questions. There must be someone who could shed light on such a strange memorial.

But neither Megan nor Will, nor anyone else, had even heard of it, let alone seen it. It took another old friend, Doctor Ivor, to come up with a particularly imaginative suggestion. The most famous GP in our part of the country, Doctor Ivor Jones was also renowned as a specialist in the arcane mysteries of Welsh bardic composition. Local history was another enthusiasm.

'The past is an open book to him' was how one of his patients put it, waiting in surgery one day. 'A proper scholar he is, never mind the flu.'

Not long afterwards, Ivor was calling at Hafod around supper-time to minister to my laryngitis. He was much more intrigued by my story of the grave.

'Borrow,' he declared over a large whisky, rubbing his balding head to stimulate further thought. 'George Borrow might give us a clue.'

We were sitting around Miss Wynne-Jones's box of books, sifting through the jumbled contents for favourites. Of course, Borrow was there. His book of travel in Wales, first published in 1862, recalls a vanished era. But to me he is still a real-life figure, striding ahead on our mountain roads in his Victorian black coat, waving his black umbrella, stopping to talk to every passer-by, talking, always talking.

'No, not *Wild Wales*,' said Ivor. 'This is the one I'm looking for, the one about the gypsies.'

Triumphantly he fished out a copy of *Lavengro*.

'There were always gypsy families travelling through these parts. I have a feeling that your Thomas Smithe – Romany spelling, by the way – might be one who departed this world while they were camping on the mountain!'

The musing and muttering went on, Ivor hunched over the pages in the lamplight like a great bespectacled owl. Eventually he came to the part he was looking for. Borrow's friend, Mr Petulengro, was describing the burial ceremony of a notorious poisoner named Mrs Herne, who hanged herself from a tree, 'being full of brimstone and the Devil's tinder'.

He rolled the words around with Cardiganshire relish. Petulengro had arrived at ' . . . the wild and desolate encampment of the Herne family. Here the dead body was laid out on a mattress in a tent, dressed Romanesk in a red cloak and big bonnet of black beaver. Early in the morning the funeral took place. The body was placed not in a coffin but on a bier and carried not to a churchyard but to a deep dell close by. And there it was buried beneath a rock, like a Romany of the old blood, the *Kosko puro rati*, brother . . . '

He closed the book, but the strange picture hung in the air. I hoped the late Mr Smithe had not been a murderer. But, thanks to the spell of Borrow, the idea of a gypsy burial had somehow been stamped on my mind and stayed there, right or wrong.

'Of course, Borrow spoke Welsh even better than he spoke Romany. Picked it up as a boy in Norfolk. And didn't he like to show off about it, the old bugger?' said Ivor. 'Still, it meant he'd got to know more about the Welsh than most of the native-born.'

'You could have filled him in about a few things, though,' I said. 'The poetry especially.' I was looking at Ivor's prescription pad on the table in front of us. Ivor had been about to write down the details of my antibiotic. But the words 'Ampicillin 250 mg' had somehow tailed off into a large heading in Welsh. '*Cynghanedd.*' Ivor had at this point been sidetracked into an explanation of a traditional rhyming form used by the old poets.

'Means harmony,' he'd gone on in some excitement. 'An ancient system of sound-chiming within each line. Like the one about Dinas Brân Castle – "The ruins now reigned over only by birds of the night!" Of course, it works better in Welsh.'

He added another dash from the whisky bottle.

'Old Manley Hopkins had a go at it, though. And he didn't do badly, did he?'

I wanted to remind dear Ivor about my prescription. But the jotting went on until the pad was full. From time to time Ivor's sonorous recitations were interrupted by his stammer, but this merely added to the rhythmical suspense. There were apparently at least a dozen kinds of poetical inspiration, all governed by the strictest of rules, even nowadays. *Englyn* was scrawled across the next page. '4-line mono-rhyme, first recorded 9th century. Similarities with Greek epigram and Japanese haiku.' *Awdl* followed, 'Long traditional poem, see first Eisteddfod, Bala, 1789.' And so the list went on through elegies and eulogies, battle-songs and wedding greetings, ending with 'Poets of the Gentry, best sung to a harp'.

'There was no such thing as unemployment for a bard,' Ivor reminded me. 'Especially in the Middle Ages. A tame one was kept by every noble household. Think of Owain Glyndŵr. Iolo Goch did him proud, didn't he? Remember the ode he wrote about the palace where Owain held court at Sycharth?'

He leaned back in his chair by the fire, waved an expansive arm.

> There dwells the Chief we all extol
> In timber house on lightsome knoll
> Upon four wooden columns proud
> Mounteth his mansion to the cloud . . .

There was a brief pause while a piece of cold sausage was consumed.

'Wasn't it Borrow who made that translation?' I put in, displaying at least a shred of scholarship. 'I remember in *Wild Wales* – '

Ivor nodded. 'And didn't he do well? What a picture!'

Well into his histrionic mode, his brown eyes were brimming with emotion as he went on . . .

> A mill, a rushing brook upon,
> And pigeon-tower framed in stone.
> A fish pond deep and dark to see
> To cast nets in when need there be.
> Of various plumage birds abound
> Herons and peacocks haunt around . . .

He brought out a large red handkerchief and blew his nose. *Wild Wales* was lying on top of Winnie's books, open at an earlier page. This was where Borrow encountered another Doctor Jones with a passion for poetry.

'Do you remember?' I asked Ivor. 'They were drinking in the pub at Cerrigydrudion, talking about a Welsh version of *Paradise Lost*. *The Loss of the Place of Bliss* was how the title was translated.'

Ivor was now finishing off some Caerphilly. 'Good, isn't it?'

I wasn't sure whether he was talking about the cheese or the title. I closed the book. 'And then Doctor Jones was summoned to attend a lady some distance away, an accouchement, it seems.'

'On call, was he?' said Ivor. He brought out a silver pocket-watch. 'Reminds me I've got to go a bit further on myself. Measles at Maesmawr. Not a good road either, especially in this weather.' He peered out at the rain lashing against the window. I imagined the Maesmawr family waiting for the headlights down the lane, and the reassurance Ivor always brought with him like a charm.

'Nearly went into the ditch coming here,' he went on. 'Damn pheasant starting up from the hedge, down by the brook. Funny thing is, it's exactly the same thing that happened to my predecessor, old Doctor Lewis, in exactly the same place. Upturned his horse and trap, but he lived to see another day all right.'

This time a dash of water went into his whisky. Ivor's own driving mishaps were legendary.

'Don't like that part of the lane anyway.'

I asked him why.

Ivor shook his head. Surely Megan had told me the tale. 'The miller's wife was drowned just below there one night, years ago. Driving the horse and cart back to the millhouse she was, in the middle of a storm. She was halfway across the river when the little bridge collapsed and she was swept away in the torrent.'

'The cartwheels were still in the field a hundred yards downstream until not long ago, just the broken pieces. I always think of it somehow, going past.'

Ivor himself lived in a millhouse of a very different kind, a sprawling cream-coloured place that dominated the crossroads, not far from the village. The handsome façade hid a labyrinth of different rooms going right back to the thirteenth-century roots of the house with its cobbled cellars, the damp whiff of the river not far below. The attics had once been a place for cockfights and somewhere beneath the polished elm staircases lurked hidden passages, supposedly used by the monks from the abbey, just a few hundred yards away. No one seemed quite sure why they needed this escape route. Ivor and Menna had other things to talk about on our evenings there, being at the heart of so much local activity. Zest for talk was what they shared. Otherwise nothing could have been more of a contrast than the solid presence of Ivor alongside the dynamic elfin figure of his wife who even spoke a different Welsh, coming from the Denbighshire mountains. It was not just his accent she teased him about either.

'The Jews of Wales these Cardys are called,' she liked to say. 'Pushy as well as mean. You know the story of the revolving doors, I suppose. Even if they're behind you going in, they're bound to be in front going out.'

Ivor laughed. 'I did have a great-grandfather called Levi, a butter-merchant from Aberystwyth way. But I think it was a name his parents picked from the Bible like they did in those days, rather than family background.'

His grandfather was a sea-captain, his father a bank manager famous for his resemblance to Neville Chamberlain. But his sons were training to be doctors, something which pleased him.

'By the way,' he was saying now, getting ready to be off again. 'You must come over again soon. Something else to show you.'

'Not more forceps!' Ivor was a great collector of medical antiques and on my last visit he demonstrated on my neck how these ancient instruments worked, a memorable experience.

'No. A priest's hidey-hole, or rather an abbot's. Griff and friends found it when they were opening up the back-parlour fireplace. Must have been as hot as hell hiding in there. Perhaps he was getting into practice!'

He handed me the prescription pad with its poetical footnotes.

'What about those English poets who came to Wales – Shelley and Wordsworth and that lot – not forgetting Peacock? He married a Welsh parson's daughter, though he left it a bit late proposing. I thought you were going to follow them up some time?'

'Some time.' It was the usual problem, I explained, the way time itself melted into thin air at Hafod.

'Well, that's paradise for you. *The Loss of the Place of Bliss*,' he quoted. He looked at me over his glasses. 'Don't you go losing yours now.'

I felt an odd twinge of foreboding. But how could such a thing ever happen?

'Mustn't forget your prescription, though,' Ivor was saying. Tugging at his pockets he brought out a syringe, then a thermometer, and finally a crumpled programme for Verdi's *Aida* in Welsh. 'This will do.'

On the back he scribbled a note to Lewis-Jones Chemist, and tucked it under the cheese-dish.

'If the bugger can't read it tell him I was in one of my bolshie moods!'

He straightened his jacket again.

'Nice suit, Ivor,' I said. I had been admiring his uncharacteristically trim appearance.

'Present from a grateful patient. Like one of those A J Cronin novels.' He gave his endearing grin. 'He'd had it made for him on holiday, he told me. It never fitted him, his wife said. So I gave him a bottle of gin by way of return. Actually,' he added, 'I've been to a hospital tea-party for the retiring dragon – sorry, matron. So that's why I'm tidy today.'

In the doorway he picked up his black bag that contained two trout wrapped in newspaper. 'Mrs Roberts's favourite. Won't take a minute on my way up the hill.'

As he was pulling on his battered waterproof and fishing hat, he remembered something else, something that made him laugh.

'When I started here as a young man I bought myself a posh coat to make me look like a proper doctor. Black it was, useful for funerals too. Got it from Merediths in the High Street in Wrexham. Remember him? He was a chap with literary leanings, all right. They used to say he must be the only gents' outfitter in the country who kept a complete Shakespeare and a *Shorter Oxford Dictionary* under the counter. Handy for reference, you see.'

I was laughing too. Ivor was halfway out but it wasn't the end of the story.

'Anyway the first case I was called out to was an old lady on a farm right at the back of beyond, somewhere between Carrog and Glyndyfrdwy. They brought me up the last part on the back of the tractor. A gynaecological problem it was, nothing serious. But I had to examine her rather intimately there and then. She was more than a bit confused in her mind but she noticed the coat all right. Just as I was going down the stairs, I heard her say to her husband, 'Well now Dilwyn, wasn't it nice of the vicar to call?'

15

A YEAR TO REMEMBER

9TH JANUARY

Woken early by strong smell of frying bacon and crash of falling masonry. Loud Welsh oaths are followed by a spate of excitable dialogue, then silence. Nailed boots crunch across slate floors on tiptoe. 'Shush!' comes a hoarse voice from just below.

Suddenly remember this is the day Griff has promised to bring up a hero of his, Idwal Tan-y-Garth, an expert on house repairs. Some urgent work is needed to save Hafod from imminent collapse, it seems. Last week R presented me with a small red notebook, saying it was time I kept a diary, if only now and again. Foreseeing an adventurous year ahead, this sounds a good idea, starting today.

Brave Siberian temperatures and mysterious power cut to struggle into dressing-gown, boots and sweaters. Halfway downstairs a heatwave greets me. Griff has produced a huge fire over which bread and eggs are now sizzling in my oldest black pan, kettle chugging alongside. Talk in the kitchen going full steam again.

'Keeping quiet we were,' Griff explains. 'So's not to disturb.'

Inside, halfway through his breakfast, is a piratical-looking young man with a bright red beard, a blue jay's feather stuck in his moleskin hat. Springs up to be introduced, doffing the moleskin (which is about to disintegrate) and hands me a mug of tea.

'As long as he takes to you, you'll be all right' is the given word about Idwal. I take to him at once. So only hope the approval is mutual.

After breakfast, Idwal whisks me out into the icy cold for a tour of inspection. Breath emerges from the beard like dragon's smoke as he expounds on plan of campaign. The way he lays a freckled hand on a crack in the wall, or a rotten door-frame somehow inspires confidence. But Idwal is a creative spirit as well as a conservationist. His eye has already lit upon the Misses Sinclair's mini sun-lounge. 'You'll want to get rid of that for a start. What you need is a proper Welsh porch – quarrystone and a slate roof. And this old bank in front' – surveying the frosted wilderness of weed and bramble – 'Steps is what you want there, big ones coming right up to the house. Somewhere to admire the view, isn't it?' Steps are obviously Idwal's passion. I see the scene in a flash, a sun-soaked terrace wreathed in honeysuckle, as he bounds up and down, arms outstretched, crackling with enthusiasm. Griff watches admiringly, nodding his bullet head. The two of them then disappear up the ladder to the gable end where a new beam is being built on. Fierce cries of instruction and counter-instruction rise up between hammer-blows. I have the feeling that Hafod has acquired a pair of unlikely guardian angels to see us through into the unknown.

12TH JANUARY

After this surge of optimism, Hafod succumbs to one of its mood swings. Today all is deserted. A positively surly atmosphere pervades the house.

No sign of the two angels as promised and the power is still off. I phone our electricity headquarters to be greeted by a voice from the depths, intoning the single word, 'Manweb!' This mystical utterance actually stands for the Merseyside and

North Wales Electricity Board. To me it always has the ring of some doom-laden druidical spell, especially today. Out of nowhere a dense grey mist has been conjured up and I am now invisible to the outside world. 'A local fault' is the verdict on the power failure. Tomorrow, possibly, someone might be available to investigate.

13TH JANUARY

The mist has sunk to the level of the river. Miraculously, Hafod is floating above it in sunshine like an emerging atoll. The paths are strung with glittering cobwebs. Soon Merlin himself, in the shape of Sammy Sparks, can be glimpsed shuttling across the valley along the spidery network of cables and wires that links us to reality.

By midday the spell has been lifted. The fault has been found and repaired and Sammy is safely back in the house.

'Time for a *paned*!' the cry goes up, rallying the rest of the commune for the ritual cuppa, Griff and Idwal from the gable end, Gwen in the spare bedroom deep in rolls of pink and white wallpaper. ('All these bulges – why did we have to choose stripes?') Within minutes the six-foot Morgan Lewis has joined us, Gwen's cousin by marriage, a highly resourceful plumber when he's not on shift at the local seed factory.

'That's all it was,' he announces, squelching through in large wellingtons. He's holding aloft a bedraggled bird's nest, fished from the outlet pipe of the ancient water-tank up in the wood. The mystery of the latest water stoppage is solved.

'That's nothing,' says Gwen. 'We had an eel stuck in our tank all summer. Must have taken a short cut up from the river.'

From eels the talk twists and turns like the Dee itself through trout-fishing, salmon-poaching, pollution scandals, and the mad English canoeists who brave the falls in bad weather. 'If they want to kill themselves, why don't they just throw themselves in,' is Idwal's opinion. Everyone laughs.

'There's plenty have done that,' pipes Sammy, *sotto voce*.

Just as swiftly, Celtic gloom descends.

'That old fellow from the Home last year, remember? He went to the river, didn't he?'

This is the way it's always put, a kind of tactful euphemism for tragedy. 'Went on the railway' is another one, rarely heard nowadays since the branch line was closed.

'Accidents is worse than suicide,' declares Griff magisterially. 'Fatal accidents, that is. My Uncle Mostyn was up in his hayloft one minute, next he'd gone for good. Missed his footing and necked himself.'

Another telling phrase, I think as I disappear upstairs. Must try to finish my script for Radio Four programme on reincarnation due to go out next week.

18TH JANUARY

Work progresses on all fronts. It occurs to me that Hafod's days as a meditative retreat are gone. The place now has touches of a Mack Sennett film, run at the wrong speed, with soundtrack added, of course. It's just a question of adjusting, I suppose.

2ND FEBRUARY

Idwal and Griff here on their own today, concreting the outside passageway. Griff's word is 'con-creating', which seems more appropriate somehow. Both are united in scorn for whoever did the job last time – 1929, according to the date cut into the old plaster.

Over a midday break (ham rolls brought up from a café where Griff has 'friends') they are in reminiscent mood. Family snapshots emerge. Griff's grandfather, for instance, was a wagoner, then a shepherd, a local character always known as The Good Man (*Y Dyn Da*).

'Why?' I ask.

'Thought he knew everything, didn't he?' is the unexpected reply. His apple cheeks crease up at the joke.

Griff's a determined bachelor and lives in a neat council

house with his father, who's a retired baker. 'As for me, I've done every job under the sun – road-mending, tree-felling, bricklaying. I'm a free man, see! And I've been to London too. Once,' he adds, 'to see the motorbike racing at Brand's Hatch. What a walk that was!'

Finding his way back to his friend's house at Shepherd's Bush in the early hours of the morning sums up Griff's picture of the metropolis. Idwal has his own view of London.

'Hell on earth for them, poor buggers, when they could be living in paradise.' He gesticulates towards the mountains which, at this moment, are rainswept. Without his hat, his red hair springs up like a burning bush. Schooldays are his indelible memory, especially the daily journey by train to Bala. 'The big lads used to get the rods out of the blinds. Beaten black and blue I was.'

Brought up on a mountain farm, he knew nothing but Welsh until he was seven. Even so, being shy, one of the worst moments at the grammar school was having to recite a nature poem in Welsh for the eisteddfod.

'*Y gwiwer!*' he says bitterly. 'Bloody squirrel!'

At least learning Latin helped with his English. But his first job couldn't come too soon. 'Got two and six a week for thrashing,' is what I think he says. Seeing my puzzled expression, he tries again. 'Going round the farms with the old threshing machine at harvest-time.' Later on he applied for agricultural college but 'came over all queer' at the exams. He lays the blame on the two enormous duck eggs served him for breakfast by a kindly farmer's wife. 'Give you strength, boy *bach*.' Anyway, there was nothing his mother and father couldn't teach him about sheep and cattle. Now he's busy helping run the farm whenever he's not working at his 'jobsies'.

'Might be courting this year, though,' he tells me later, hurrying off to do the evening milking.

'Marriage,' snorts Griff. He slaps his shiny red tractor. 'I'm happy enough with this one, I can tell you!'

Together they make their departure into the wintry dusk, Idwal bouncing ahead in his yellow van which is strangely painted with black spots.

'The Cheetah they call me. So everyone can see me coming!'

10TH FEBRUARY

The day Idwal throws the Misses Sinclair's 1930s fireplace down the mountain. Another symbol of modernity bites the dust as the sun-porch is uprooted and hurled away in its wake. Unfortunately, this is the moment Dr Ivor is turning up the track in our direction. Narrowly escapes the unexpected landslide, which should add another chapter to his motoring sagas. Luckily Idwal is a friend (originally recommended to us by Ivor). So all ends amiably over kitchen tea, fortified with brandy for the survivor.

13TH FEBRUARY

The hole in the dining-room wall has been excavated to reveal a five-foot-deep cave. No sign of a beam, alas, but Idwal takes me to a farmhouse in his valley that is being 'refurbished'. Owner and wife just off to a funeral but seem happy enough for Idwal to carry away a battered oak specimen that has been thrown into the barn. On the way back he tells me that the word has gone out in Llangollen that 'Hafod are rebuilding!' As usual in Wales, something of an exaggeration, but strikes the right note of drama.

19TH FEBRUARY

Birds are another of Idwal's passions. Today I find him halfway up a Scots pine at the back of the house tearing down an old magpie's nest. 'Or they'll be back in the spring for you. Your chaffinches and warblers won't want to build with them around, I can tell you.'

A RAM IN THE WELL

Fireplace plastering completed and an iron canopy installed with a high-barred grate, big enough to take the mightiest of Griff's logs. Both have been made by a blacksmith friend of Idwal's called Arthur, rightly known as King Arthur. All is framed by the newly polished beam, that looks as if it has always been there.

27TH FEBRUARY

Griff, Idwal and self gather for the ceremonial lighting of the first fire. Will it 'draw'? That is the vital question. At first it blazes up bravely. Then suddenly smoke billows out. Coughing and cursing the infernal powers with many a *Diawl* and an *Uffern*, Idwal dashes outside while Griff is instructed to lay on fresh fuel. Following on Idwal's heels, I watch in horror as he clambers onto the roof, with an axe in his hand. The next minute there is a loud crack and the old black chimney cowl is removed as neatly as the top of an egg. A plume of smoke rises into the air. With cries of triumph we rush inside to find the fire in its element, flames surging upwards under the canopy. 'Draught,' explains Idwal. 'It'll always go for you now, this one.' The two of them collapse, sooty-faced, on the settle to toast success with a whisky.

1ST MARCH

St David's Day. A tattered Welsh dragon flies from the gable end. Home for the week, R is taken on as builder's mate as work progresses on the new porch. A splendid structure is beginning to rise from the stack of old stone brought up from the debris of the nearby barn. 'Abbey stones, some of these,' Idwal says, handling them with respect. Holding the ladder, R is unlucky enough to receive one of them on his head. Deflected by his Beatle cap, it's caught by him on its second bounce, as it were. Idwal displays admiration. 'Fair play to him, he moved well!' A sprained hand and a bruised head could perhaps cause problems in court, though. We suggest Idwal write a note explaining that R might have to be off work for a few days. This missive from I Jones, Builder, to E Jones, Employer, is duly made out. No doubt will be much appreciated by our good friend Elwyn Jones, the Lord Chancellor.

15TH MARCH

Porch walls completed, rising to a peak with slates from the quarry. All that is needed is a solid floor to match. Will Pen-y-Bryn kindly offers us a much-prized slab enshrined in the farm's old *ty bach* and now visited only by the hens. So another piece of history is to be added to the Hafod jigsaw.

21ST MARCH

Down in the wagon to collect our floor, past fields that are full of bounding lambs and weary mothers. Will looks weary too. Has had a bad chest and is taking a break by the fire, silver specs on his nose, loaf and teapot on the table, Jethro at his feet. Idwal and Griff disappear to load up the slab. Megan asks me if I know about *spleisio*. 'Means splicing. Come and see!'

In the shed is a minute baby lamb, an orphan, standing on wobbly legs, almost swamped by what looks like an extra fur coat, complete with tail. The only way to get it 'adopted', Megan explains, is to find a bereaved ewe. But that isn't good enough. The coat of her own deceased offspring has to be removed and fastened around the impostor before she will even let it come near.

A flustered-looking ewe is brought in.

'She's all right now. It's the smell, you see.'

As we watch, the stepmother licks and the lamb begins to feed.

'Will's the one who does it,' Megan says with pride 'Has a special needle and thread to sew the coat round tight, while I hold it still.' She smiles tenderly. 'Worth it, though, isn't it?'

Back at Hafod, the slab is propped up in the porch. Idwal's in a hurry to get back to his own lambing. There are about a hundred new arrivals, with fifty more to come.

'I'm on call till midnight, see. After that my mother and father take it in turn to sit up by the fire in case they're needed. They go out round the fields at three, then again at five, and they're up for the day at seven.'

'You too?' I ask.

'Getting me out of bed in the morning is Shep's job – my best dog. Always goes down to the brook to wash his paws before he comes upstairs . . . '

10TH APRIL

The valley is a dream of beauty, veiled in a pale golden light, the air soft with new scents – hawthorn, bluebells, primroses. Back from London to rest weary wits after strenuous but enjoyable new series of interviews with couples such as the Muggeridges and the Healeys. The Cheetah is at the gate though, so fresh challenges await. Inside the path is barred by a six-foot-high molehill, out of which pokes a familiar moleskin hat and red beard. Foundations for the steps, Idwal explains. With a bow, he hands me the spade to make the first incision, then brings out a scribbled scrap of paper. 'Two flights there'll be, like this, see. L-shaped with a what-d'ye-call in the middle. Landing, I mean!' He grins. 'The cocktail patio that'll be, I suppose?'

Seeing my expression, he relents, points out the ancient moss-covered steps lurking in other corners of the garden. 'Don't worry, they'll look like those soon enough. And wait till you see this!'

Up the banks at the back of the house a series of narrow stairways has been dug into the soil and neatly edged in timber. So there are now dusky tunnels winding through right to the top of the wood.

'Griff did them last week,' Idwal tells me. 'Huw Half-a-Day helped.' This is another mutual friend, so called on account of his eccentric working hours. Only the owl is displeased, tucked away with his back to us in the fork of the oak. Late that night he voices his protest in no uncertain terms.

Hafod will have a grand total of 93 outside steps old and new. In between counting them, I admire the slate cutting skills of both Idwal and Griff as they finish off the lengths brought over from the quarry. All I do is wield the occasional tape-measure and pencil. Warm sunshine shimmers down. Gwen gives me a pruning demonstration on the old cabbage roses now soaring skywards. From the wood the first cuckoo chimes in with blackbird's arpeggios. Mozart's harp and flute faintly on the radio – one of those moments when all things seem to be part of a mysterious whole.

Step-making almost finished. When it rains, Idwal retreats to the bench he has made in the porch, watches the downpour impatiently, dashing out in every interval. I bring out our Fijian mats to cover the mortar in case of night frosts. Find in the morning that the brightly-coloured patterns have attracted some early butterflies, poised in surprise amongst the pink hibiscus and woven messages of the makers, Litia and Lora.

In the afternoon even more startling, a brilliant, three-foot butterfly appears. It's carried up the path by Morgan's brother, Hywel, who's making models for tourists (and locals) to decorate the outside of houses. He's an adventurous rolling stone and this latest enterprise seems to be flourishing.

Death sentence has been pronounced on the stricken elm by the gate. The three Thomas brothers, celebrated tree-fellers, arrive to take charge, joined by the home team, Griff and

Idwal and Huw Half-a-Day – a chubby cheerful character – with Dewi the Post as interested bystander.

'Up you go, lad!' the eldest Thomas instructs a skinny fifty-year-old.

Vanishing heavenwards, a face peers out, ears hidden in leaves. He seems to be looking for R.

'Is the gentleman out of the way?'

He is, but not the lady, who finds herself engulfed in foliage as the topmost branches fall to the chainsaw.

'Women and children not allowed at tree-fellings,' says Thomas Senior, steering me into the porch.

A steel hawser is fastened round the base. Violent tug-of-war ensues to awful wrenchings and groanings. Unbelievably the tree begins to lurch down the wrong way. The house seems to cringe. Shouts and cries of dismay. Then the tractor pulls it back. It swerves in the other direction, finally crashes down against the mountainside.

All gather for a tea-drinking wake around the fallen giant. Young Thomas estimates its age at a hundred and fifty. Amidst the sawing and clearing, I spot a survivor, a baby wood-dove cowering in the remains of the family nest. Transferred to a cardboard box, Humphrey (so called) turns up his beak at my efforts to provide nourishment. Not surprising, as all I can find in the way of a feeding bottle is Dr Grimshaw's Nasal Douche, a sinister-looking relic of the Misses Sinclair's medicine cupboard.

16TH MAY

Humphrey's box is empty, although carefully camouflaged in foliage by kind-hearted Griff. Perhaps the parents returned for a rescue operation. More likely, the ever-watchful buzzard enjoyed an early breakfast. One elm inhabitant is still at home. A diminutive shrew emerges from a hole in the stump, pauses to wash behind his ears then hurries off on urgent business, hopping like a kangaroo.

A Year to Remember

The Thomas trio return with the JCB and start to excavate the gap in the mountainside where the tree came down. I prepare for an avalanche. Instead, an impressive clearing appears where vehicles can turn and park at the end of the nerve-racking climb up to Hafod. Griff digs in a line of stones to mark the edge. Politely suggests that a coat of white paint might be a help to those guests who've been 'enjoying a drink or two'. Brother Renfrey on one of his Sunday visits agrees with this – might even be persuaded drive his prehistoric Volvo up instead of leaving it at the farm.

23RD JUNE

The steps are complete. '*Bendigedig!*' Idwal exclaims (meaning blessed, according to the hymn-books). A special path has been designed by him to lead up to them. This afternoon he brings up a load of small greeny-grey pebbles fresh from the river-bed, spreads them ankle-deep in his enthusiasm. Crunching along my new path this evening I'm back again on the shingle beaches of childhood holidays – a magical illusion.

15TH JULY

Dear Graham, the first of our summer regulars, is a late riser. Sound of smoker's cough alerts me to make black coffee. Snatches of *Rigoletto* from the bathroom. Our hedonistic friend of South Sea days, ex-broadcaster now teaching in Saudi, is not as happy as he sounds though.

'I may have to see a doctor,' he says, emerging in flowing kaftan. 'I think I may be going deaf.'

'Surely not.' I carry on scrambling eggs. 'Just the hangover, I expect.'

He shakes his head. 'Awful buzzing in my ears, on and off all night. Read somewhere it's a sure sign. Or else a brain tumour.'

Fate is kind. Idwal has appeared to repair bedroom

window-catches. Next minute there's a muffled shout from Graham's room.

'Bees!'

'Bees?'

We pound upstairs. There's nothing to see but the whole room throbs with a huge, angry humming.

'Like a bloody aerodrome,' as Idwal says. He's crouched down behind the bed where the fireplace has been sealed up for years. 'Swarmed in the chimney, they have.'

Huge relief on Graham's plump face. The prospect of imminent deafness vanishes. Cheerfully moves his belongings to the other side of the house while Griff and Half-a-Day crowd in to debate the crisis.

'Burn them out?'

'Drown them out?'

'Ring the Agricultural.'

No offers. 'Can't get them out of a chimney,' they tell us.

Half-a-Day concurs with this. The Royal Hotel, which he knows well, has had a Bee Chimney for years. 'In the end they had to close up the room.'

Which is what we do, for the time being at least. Tomorrow is another day.

16TH JULY

Idwal's brainwave. Lewis-Jones Chemist has unearthed a particularly powerful wasp-spray from the cellar. Armed with this, Idwal makes a slit in the plywood over the grate and discharges the contents up the chimney. All retreat as the furious buzzing rises to a crescendo, then dies away.

Within hours the path below is littered with corpses. Idwal opens up the grate and removes remaining shovelfuls of the invaders.

Graham is now worried about bats. Says he has seen them fluttering round the eaves of his new quarters. Fortunately his knowledge of wildlife is limited. Seems reassured when I persuade him it's a favourite nesting-place for the swallows.

5TH AUGUST

The team embarks on what is to be known as the Great Wall of Hafod, a system of defence-works designed to keep out both the mountain and the sheep. Summer visitors much impressed by what they take to be age-old Celtic skills with dry stones. In fact, barrowloads of mortar are involved and endless reinforcements of posts and sheep-wire.

Griff gets on well with our friends, especially the eccentric six-foot-four Merryne, a one-time director of agriculture, with many a tale of his years spent under the African sun. Sitting out on the steps, there is animated talk of weeds and fertilizers and Griff's prize-winning beetroots. Cheese sandwiches are consumed while favourite tools are demonstrated, a mighty sledge-hammer and an iron 'hook' for the grass. Another distinguished guest, Colonel Rodie, who's used to more formal ways, is somewhat surprised perhaps to be presented at breakfast with a comradely jar of pickled onions. 'Home-made, they are,' Griff assures him. 'You'll never taste better.'

Idwal is in demand with enthusiastic BBC producers who come to stay. Tape recorders are set up to capture tales of the rural past but Idwal is strangely reluctant to preserve himself for posterity. There's plenty of repartee when Vanessa's young actor friends from television are with us, though. And, if our visitors are writers, at least they disappear to jot down Idwal's stories in private.

20TH AUGUST

According to Mrs Roberts it's the worst drought since 1911, or even 1921. 'This Global Warning it is.' The weeks of heatwave have certainly coincided with some curious events. A little while ago there was a small earthquake. 'Several sheep injured,' reported the Pwllheli newspaper.

'Nearly threw me out of bed,' is Idwal's version of the strange tremors and rumblings. Then there was a Wagnerian thunderstorm which produced an awesome spectacle of *son et lumière* around our valley. Next day a bolt of lightning struck a neighbouring church and set it on fire. Finally, this morning Griff reports sighting a UFO through his bedroom window. 'A huge bright light it was, right over the Berwyns.'

Half-a-Day suggests it might have something to do with the ten port-and-lemons he boasted of consuming that evening. But Griff is adamant. He's seen it other nights too. All he needs is to borrow R's binoculars to get a closer look.

'Mind the aliens don't come to get you,' chaffs Idwal.

But Griff thinks all these things might well mean the beginning of the end of the world. I prefer the idea of the second coming of Glyndŵr heralded, like his birth, by supernatural signs and wonders.

'Fiery shapes' burned in the heavens, and the earth 'shak'd like a coward'. According to Shakespeare anyway.

3RD SEPTEMBER

And now the mountain is on fire. Or rather has been. I've been away working at the BBC, recording memories of the sun-scorched deserts of the Yemen. The heat in London seemed to rise to Aden temperatures. I imagine Wales as a green oasis as R and I drive back together. Not so. There's a red glow in the sky over Eglwyseg as we get near home and the mist in the valley looks like smoke. In the half-light the slopes are patched with black. Thank God, in the distance, Hafod stands white and untouched.

'Yes, there's been a bit of a fire,' they tell us at the farm. 'No danger now. Just the end of it up on the moors.'

Apparently it started three days ago along the top of Fron, a dropped match in the bracken, they think. Idwal and the rest went out beating, trying to divert water from the well but it was too low. At one time flames were springing up again towards Hafod. The fire-brigade were away with fires on the next mountain. So Will and Owen joined in to dig a trench right round the outside fence. Howard came from Wrexham with friends to help. 'We all agreed not to worry you, ringing London,' Megan says. (Worry is an understatement here, I thought). Then yesterday the wind dropped and the fire died out. Just this morning, the Forestry Warden has been round the whole of Fron Fawr in his Land rover and reported no sign of any new outbreaks. Besides, there is rain due at last.

As we go into the house the first drops fall. Inside, a fine black dust coats everything. A bitter scorched smell still hangs on the air. On the table there are two notes, one from Howard, the other from Griff in his usual capitals. 'FIRE OUT WE WERE HERE.'

It's a reassuring message. We know that mountain fires are a common thing in North Wales in a dry season. But I suppose we like to think that Hafod is under some divine protection. Or is it? Suddenly, for the first time, our frailty is exposed, in more ways than one. Tonight, for once, it's hard to sleep . . .

20TH SEPTEMBER

As usual, a major drama is followed by a minor one, just to keep us on the alert. This time the focus of interest is the cattle-grid. It's being built at Will's instigation to replace the awkward old gate at the end of the track, also to stop stray sheep getting through from the mountain. Carrying out the construction is one Moses Price, a distant cousin of Megan and Gwyneth. He's a short red-faced man with bulging eyes, one of those known as a 'character', which can be a word of warning. More important, there are rumours of an ancestral feud with Idwal Tan-y-Garth, something to do with the mysterious diversion of a stream from one farm to another. As a result, Idwal and The Cheetah have been denied access to the track by Mr Price until work is completed. This rouses

Idwal to a fury as he is in the middle of bringing up vital parts for a new water-tank. A judicial inquiry is requested which takes place on site in Idwal's absence. Mr Price is polite but stands his ground as an expert witness.

Mr P: 'Can't be responsible, *Syr*, if Tan-y-Garth drives over it when the cement is set.'

R: 'What if some planks are put over the hole?'

Mr P: 'Cause terrible damage, *Syr*. You see it's here *forever*, the grid, isn't it?'

R: 'Even some temporary cover, a tarpaulin perhaps?'

Mr P: 'Is it a matter of life and death for Tan-y-Garth?' (A trump card.)

R: 'Not really, Mr. Price.'

Mr P (triumphant): 'Then let it settle, *Syr*. For God's sake, let it settle, isn't it?'

So the frontier post remains closed. But the use of a wheelbarrow along the side path is to be permitted, thanks to a diplomatic settlement with Pen-y-Bryn.

5TH OCTOBER

Hafod harvest festival. Find a lavish arrangement of produce assembled on the kitchen table, a giant marrow as centrepiece surrounded by potatoes, onions, broad beans, lettuce and, of course, beetroot. Griff scowls at the very idea of my paying for this largess from his garden. 'Plenty more where that came from.'

He's walked up today to 'break in' his new boots. Horse mushrooms are added to the pile, still warm from the sun, picked from the fields while he's been working on the pot-holes in the track. Autumn is Griff's season. Even now he's delving into his pockets for a handful of hazelnuts which he collects like a squirrel and cracks ferociously between his teeth. Soon it will be time for bonfires, raking up the leaves and hurling out rubbish from the sheds – all pleasurable occupations. If there's something he doesn't like doing he's quite good at becoming hard of hearing, or there's the classic postponement, 'That's for the back end of the year, see.'

Meanwhile, if it's raining, he's happy padding round the house in his socks, cleaning the tiny upstairs windows vigorously enough to crack one or two. So that's the next job anyway.

20TH OCTOBER

Idwal's absence is explained by the news that he's been busy getting married. His wife is called Mary, a charming and statuesque young woman he met playing badminton.

She is not Welsh-speaking nor from a farming family either. It's reliably reported by local spies though that the honeymoon was spent on the farm, that the morning after the wedding Idwal was up to do the milking as usual, and the bride was out in the field cutting thistles. Certainly bears out his claim that 'she's a grand little worker'. Generally thought to be a calming influence on the wild Welshman.

5TH NOVEMBER

While Idwal is setting up in his new house, a replacement is brought up by Griff. Unlike our regulars, Caradoc is a solemn man, a tall, lean figure with a vague air of dignity about him. I am not surprised when he hands me a rather worn card that tells me he's a 'Restorer of Ancient Monuments'. He has certainly come to the right place although the first jobs he carries out are simple enough. Cigarette in hand, pencil behind one ear, he spends the day stripping the two 'modern' doors down to the tongue-and-groove originals. Also promises to bring up some old brass knobs, 'next time', and do some patching at the back of the family settle, date 1649. Relaxes later over a whisky to confide in us that he too is planning matrimony.

'I've known her since we were in school – must be forty years ago. But it's been a bit sudden, this idea of fixing a day . . .'

A Ram in the Well

Guy Fawkes crackers and rockets over the village strike a celebratory note.

Griff is highly indignant about a missing ladder. Caradoc has also gone missing. Griff puts two and two together. 'Well, that's one thing he can restore anyway, the bugger. Doesn't need a ladder to get married, does he?'

Message received that the ladder has only been 'borrowed'. Will be returned safely 'next time'. But I can't help feeling that the Restorer was only a temporary addition to Hafod.

Idwal is back in the fold with an invitation to tea at Tan-y-Garth. This is a memorable occasion, Idwal driving me over in the afternoon. Outside the farm, a solid nineteenth-century house, half a dozen dogs rush out to greet us, each one chained to a barrel that is a kennel. Only Shep is allowed in with us.

The parlour-kitchen, papered with roses, is the heart of the house, table crammed with cakes and scones, plates of cold ham and potatoes simmering on the Aga 'just in case'. Idwal's mother bustles to and fro, talking at the top of her voice. B and B guests from England call her the Shepherdess, on account of her skills with her flocks. But nothing could be further from the Dresden image. 'Big Rhian' suits her better. Idwal's father is a small twig-like man with formal manners, much concerned to know if 'the lad' has been of any use to us up at Hafod.

No sooner have extra supplies been brought up from Mary's new house, than I'm told that Tom and Ceinwen are expecting me 'if you've got time'. More greetings from Idwal's auntie and uncle at their house up the hill, currently being repaired. This is the Uncle Tom who's known to be 'brainy'. A gaunt, impressive man, he's famous for the scope of his curses when training his dogs.

He's something of an autocrat too. At Idwal's request he demonstrates how he summons the family to meals on his First World War bugle. The red-haired Ceinwen responds with a few tremulous chords on the family harp in the corner ('should get it tuned, shouldn't I?') while Tom discusses the Latin origin of some peculiar Welsh place-names ('Bonwm, for instance. Certain to mean *bonum*, a good place, from when the Romans were here.')

It's difficult to tear myself away from such entertainments. 'Sorry about the scaffolding,' Ceinwen says as I'm leaving. She can't resist telling me about the day the first iron bar went through the upstairs wall. 'Then right through the wardrobe, and out into the bedroom. Which was a bit of a shock for my mother's sister who was having a lie-in with a cup of tea. But that's these old houses for you . . . '

9TH DECEMBER

My last day of the year at Hafod and the last page of the red notebook. Sadly we have to be in London for Christmas and January too. So yesterday Griff and Idwal were here battening down the hatches – pipes lagged, doors and windows sealed against draughts and mice, bag of road-salt at the ready by the gate. All the building work that's been done up here seems to have put new life into the house. There's even a new view, the valley below framed in the stone archway of Idwal's porch.

'Everything shipshape,' is the way Griff put it as we said goodbye.

As usual, Idwal has the last line. 'Don't hang around,' he warned me with a wink. 'That bloody planning inspector's been round these parts lately, poking his nose into things – the English one with the glasses.'

Perhaps it was only a joke. Nevertheless I feel the urge to be on my way. No chance of a lift with Will or Owen as it's market day. But it is Tuesday. Have already sighted the bus on its way into town, steamily lit up against the December gloom. Soon it will be back on the last round trip, hastening down into Llan in time for Trevor's *Messiah* rehearsals. In time for the last train too with any luck.

I pull out my boots and umbrella. Once again it's the Why-Walk to the rescue . . .

16

MEMORIALS

Fortunes change. Houses change. Almost overnight a way of life can vanish for good. But not here, I would say to myself, looking out from Hafod on another green morning. Behind the house the rowan tree was thick with berries again after its brush with fire that summer of the heatwave. In our hidden valley everything seemed as immutable as the surrounding mountains.

I had forgotten about death. Within a few years of each other, two of those closest to us at Hafod were suddenly gone. One was Philip Yorke, the other Will Pen-y-Bryn. Deaths like these seem to mark some kind of rift in time, part of the apparently endless present swallowed up into the past.

With the removal of two such familiar figures from the landscape of my life, that landscape itself is subtly altered. It is like a break in the weather. After a long spell of golden sunshine there were threatening skies, even over Hafod. Looking ahead, I found the future had somehow slipped out of focus. Nothing was certain any more. In a strange way I seemed to be no longer in charge of what was happening to me. In London R's workload was increasing and, at the BBC, there was talk of a new direction to my own career. How long could I take the strain of this tug-of-war between such different loyalties? In the end would

Hafod be the casualty, Wales itself abandoned as an impossible dream?

Perhaps it was this growing sense of uncertainty that made the memories of our two friends so important. Philip and Erddig were, of course, inseparable. But there were later pictures too. Almost a year had gone by since the handover to the National Trust. In that time he had moved from an empty property on the estate to the tiny terraced house that was 'so handy for fish and chips'. Visitors like us who still called on him there would find him as busy with repairs as he had been at Erddig, up a ladder slating the roof or painting the porch an eccentric blue. Yet now there was the sad air of the remittance man about him, an exile from home even though that home was only a few miles away. Secretly perhaps the heart had gone out of him. The days of tea-parties in the Servants' Hall were over. So were the village concerts with his father's magic lantern and his musical saw.

But he was still Squire Yorke as he unfailingly made his rounds of the local churches for Sunday services. On that last afternoon he cycled to one of his favourite places, little Penylan, deep in the countryside between Erddig and Llangollen. It was a hot July day. Somewhat breathless, he arrived late and slipped into an empty pew at the back. There he was found at the end of the service. It was his second stroke and he died instantly, with a characteristic sense of time and place. He was seventy-three.

The funeral at the family church at nearby Marchwiel was as crowded and traditional as one would expect. But it was another occasion, four years later, that somehow stays in the memory. A commemorative plaque was to be dedicated at a special service. Country flowers filled the eighteenth-century blue and white interior. Those who'd come to pay tribute ranged from village people and elderly tenants to National Trust gentry in Sunday pinstripes and a remarkable thespian contingent, led by the veteran actress in scarlet and green and the ever-faithful Heyhoe.

MEMORIALS

As ever, the Marquess of Anglesey dominated the scene, bear-like in an ancient tweed jacket. A carefree rent in the sleeve was revealed as he raised an arm to recite the dedication to 'Philip Yorke, Actor and Last Squire of Erddig'. 'A Loyal Churchman', the epitaph continued. Apparently the phrase 'lay reader' could not be used as it seems this function had been performed by Phil without formal licence.

'How amused he would be by that,' said someone next to me. The archdeacon and the rector conducting the service did their best to recapture that unique figure. It wasn't really necessary. We all had him firmly in our imaginations as the village choirboys in purple and white led us in the singing of his favourite hymn, 'Fight The Good Fight'. It was the perfect metaphor, if one were needed, for all those years of struggle to save Erddig.

The marble tablet was carved by the famous Welsh sculptor, Jonah Jones, another striking figure in his multi-coloured blazer. Alongside it were lined all the other Yorke memorials, including a eulogy to the first Philip of the Gainsborough portrait.

. . . Farewell, lamented Shade,

No discord e'er disturbed thy placid mind
To every sound of woe thy heart inclined . . .

It summoned up my own Philip, too, I thought, as I stood in front of it afterwards . . . 'A kind benevolence its own reward . . . '

With me was an old solicitor friend who, as registrar, was responsible for examining the family vault before the interment of the last Squire. The caskets were in poor condition, he told me with pleasurable Welsh melancholy. He nodded towards the female figure carved on the next memorial.

'Poor Anne Jemima. Just a few bones and a hank of hair.'

'Red hair?' I asked.

'Not red,' he said reprovingly. 'Chestnut, and as bright as ever . . . '

For both Philip and Will Pen-y-Bryn, death came in a way they would perhaps have chosen, one in church, the other out in the valley. Will's was just as swift too, a heart attack while he was cutting wood with his brother from one of their trees. He was sixty-seven. We were in London when Gwen rang to give us the news. We stood in the kitchen, trying to take it in. Just the day before I had been at Hafod. Will came out from the door of the farm as I made my way down to catch the bus on the other side of the hill.

'Off to London again?'

'Just for a week.'

'Not long then.'

His voice was consoling, the blue eyes shrewd as he watched my expression. Inside I changed into the boots I had left there, put by Megan to warm by the fire. The ice on the lane was only just starting to melt under the salt.

'I'll drive you to the top,' said Will, taking down his cap from its hook on the door. No need, I told him. I only had a small bag of papers to carry. Besides, I wanted to stop at Pant Glas with a message about eggs and a book for Mrs Roberts.

Now all that placid family life was split apart by grief. I remembered last year Owen's saying, 'The spring's gone out of him a bit.' That was after a minor heart attack, again out working in the bitter weather. But no one was prepared for this calamity.

The funeral was fixed for the following Monday. But there was no way we could be there for it. R was in court and I had a week's live broadcasting to carry out for *Woman's Hour*. Both of us were dreading the drive into the valley when we eventually got back to Wales. Outside the tumbledown witch's cottage by the stream was the clearing where Will and Owen were so often to be seen, as they were that day, loading logs around the old tree-stump. We went past quickly. At the two farms the lights were on in the bedrooms, but the downstairs windows were dark and the dogs were silent.

The next day R brought the two sisters up in the car. Megan was pale and stooping, unfamiliar in her widow's coat and hat, Gwyneth's hand on her arm as they came up the path. There were tearful embraces. After tea around the fire, they went through the sad litany of Will's end as they must have done so often over the past two weeks.

'That dinner-time he was so restless. Wanted to get back to work with Owen straight away . . .' Her voice trailed off.

'They talked to each other on the phone at least three or four times a day,' Gwyneth put in. 'Even though they'd be seeing each other the next minute.'

'Only that morning he'd moved the blanket-chest in the parlour to where you could see it better. He was so proud of it.'

'We all thought since he'd given up the cattle he seemed to be taking it easy a bit.'

Megan's eyes were on the window and the view of the lane running down between the farms. 'Bethan's two boys, Aled and David, came straight away. Brought him home on the tractor.'

'Owen was up at Pant Glas ringing for Doctor Ivor. But it was too late. He'd gone on the instant.'

The funeral had been extraordinary, they said. Little Bethesda was so full, people were standing out in the lane to join in the hymns even if they couldn't hear the minister's eulogy. In a few weeks' time there was to be a presentation in his memory by the Sunday School children, just a small occasion. They knew R would be back in London but they would like it if I could be there.

I had been in the chapel before. I remembered the varnished pine pews and the smell of polish, the severe white walls and the gold-painted Bible texts above the pulpit. It was the coldest day of spring, inside and out. The plain glass windows were streaked with rain and from the nearby fields the cries of the new lambs could be heard, plaintive and shivery. Inside, a dozen children in best clothes sat up straight and solemn in the front, Will's family behind them – Megan with Gwyneth and Bethan, the two husbands, and the grown-up children. I was with friends from the surrounding farms and cottages who were gathered further back.

I knew Will had been a deacon and precentor at Bethesda, like his father before him. But I had no sense of his presence until the young teacher who was taking the service read out the lesson for the day. It was the story of Joseph and the coat of many colours. When she came to the line about the brothers 'guarding their sheep in the fields', a tremor ran through the chapel as if a nerve had been touched. At the last words, 'Behold, this dreamer cometh,' an image came to my mind of that wry, gentle expression of Will's, shaking his head at the follies of the modern world.

Afterwards, the children read out a Welsh translation of the famous speech by Martin Luther King. 'I have a dream . . . ' I was wondering why until the teacher spoke up again with a catch in her voice.

'We all have a dream today, the dream of a Wales whose language and traditions live on as they did for Mr Davis.'

A small girl came up to the family to present the 'Testament', a bible inscribed in memory of Will with a verse composed in his honour. A neighbouring farmer stood up to deliver a dignified vote of thanks, mentioning Will's special pride in the choir's successes. He nodded towards the silver shield on the window ledge, one of the chapel's few adornments. When the organ sounded for the last hymn, I saw Owen, in his brown raincoat, brace his shoulders for this most emotional of moments. But his bass voice rang out as true and steady as if his brother were singing next to him.

Finally it was question-time for the children, a Sunday School ritual that was always included, whatever the occasion. Asked about the Bible lesson, they were suddenly tongue-tied with shyness. A grandmother next to me sighed.

'That's country children all over. They know the answers well enough. How are they going to manage in the world today?'

Just for a moment, today's world was far away. Inside the chapel it could have been a Sunday afternoon a hundred years ago. In truth, Bethesda itself was rumoured to be listed for close-down, to be swept away as its rival had been and the row of workmen's cottages beyond. As we walked out, the weekend motorbikes were revving up on the Pass, shattering the calm of the village below. In spite of the onslaught of progress, though, it seemed to me the valley was determined to survive, its handful of original families mixed in with the hopeful newcomers, some with local links, others with none. Only time would tell if the place still had a real heart to it.

Mrs Roberts, as usual, was optimistic when I called at Pant Glas later in the week.

'The farms are the life-blood of this part of Wales. As long as they flourish, so will the valley.'

Even in the midst of change, she looked as much of a fixture as ever, sitting bolt upright in her usual armchair by the fire. Only the red-rimmed eyes behind the glasses betrayed the shock of losing Will, and the worry over Megan's health that had followed it. Today she'd gone with Bethan to the hospital for a check-up, Gwyneth told me.

'Will she stay on at Pen-y-Bryn?' I asked.

No one really knew yet, it seemed. When she was well enough, she might move to a little house in Llangollen for a change of scene.

'Pero would go with her, of course. Back to being a town dog again.'

We all smiled at that. At Pen-y-Bryn young David was to take on the sheep and bring over some of the cattle from the Pandy farm. There was talk that he might get married before long.

'As for us, we'll be on the move too, quite soon.' Mrs

Roberts raised her hands heavenwards. 'Me at my age!' she said with her wry little laugh. 'The packing up doesn't bear thinking about.'

We looked around at the huge old dresser with its rows of willow-pattern, at the oak table and the grandfather clock, all seemingly rooted forever on the flagstone floor. It was true then that Owen was giving up some of his livestock, taking on a smaller place a couple of miles away. My heart sank. I was trying to imagine the two farms without a familiar figure at the door, the talk and the *paned* waiting inside.

'Not far away, though, is it?' Gwyneth said gently. 'And on the way into town.'

Mrs Roberts put her hand over mine. 'Well, you'll still be up at Hafod, anyway, that's for sure.'

I found myself silent, unable to reassure her. Gwyneth was quick to change the subject.

'What are you writing about at the moment – more stories from Wales? What about the Ladies of Llangollen? You've been to the house, of course, Plas Newydd?'

I had indeed and failed to find fresh inspiration in that much-told saga of the two runaway heiresses from Ireland who achieved lifelong bliss in their idyllic retreat. The admirable book by Elizabeth Mavor recounts their time there in every detail from 1780 onwards. But somehow for me the dust had settled on the celebrated eccentricities of Lady Eleanor Butler and the Hon Sarah Ponsonby. In fact, exploring the nooks and crannies of their oak-encrusted home, I experienced not just acute claustrophobia but the strong sense that I was *de trop*, one of those uninvited visitors they were so determined to repel – and rightly. Today's tourists, no doubt, would be the last straw.

But Gwyneth was more impressed. 'All those great people from England who travelled here to meet them! You know that Wordsworth called one day?'

'Yes, and was never invited again. All because his poem about them described the house as a "low-roofed cott"!'

'Poetic licence, I suppose,' said Mrs Roberts knowledgeably. 'He wrote a good one about climbing Snowdon though, didn't he? I remember we had to learn a bit at school.'

So did we. Winnie never tired of extolling those stanzas from *The Prelude*, while reminding us that, had it not been for the youthful Wordsworth's visit to his Welsh undergraduate friend, Robert Jones, in the Vale of Clywd, such a work might not exist. My own favourite had been the one about the shepherd's dog unearthing a hedgehog in the rocks. But now I was more interested in Shelley's stay in North Wales. Just the other day I'd come across some pages of the dog-eared typescript of the book I'd tried writing about his marriage to poor Harriet who was only sixteen. I was nineteen at the time and soon to be married myself which gave me, as I thought, a special insight into that reckless relationship. Needless to say, happiness and domestic incompetence soon put paid to the idea of recreating Harriet's tragedy and most of the pages ended up in the laundry basket with R's unironed shirts.

'I'd like to go to Tremadoc,' I said. 'He stayed at a house there called Tan-yr-Allt, planning to raise funds for William Madocks's great embankment scheme. That was the idea anyway. But then he claimed someone had tried to murder him. So the next day he and his wife made off for Dublin and never went back.'

'Dear me!' declared Mrs Roberts. 'I shouldn't think so!'

'You should go there, though,' Gwyneth said. She laughed. 'The Why-Walk doesn't get that far, but there's plenty of other buses.'

As I left she gave me an unexpected kiss. 'Besides, you're looking a bit *digalon* these days. The trip will do you good.'

17

THINGS RECREATED

It was true that I needed a distraction from depressing thoughts. The possibility of time running out for me at Hafod was weighing on my mind. Perhaps the book on Harriet could be resurrected, I thought, as I set out a few days later.

A solitary pilgrimage was what I had in mind, a romantic communing with the Shelley ghosts in Tan-yr-Allt that now stood empty, or so I had been told.

How wrong were my informants! Dropped off by the bus at Tremadoc, Madocks's extraordinary little model town of the early 1800s, I started to make my way up a winding drive to the house. The mountain views looked promisingly poetical, so did the ancient woods with their dark, overhanging trees.

> Woods to whose depths retired to die
> The wounded Echo's melancholy,
> And whither this lone spirit bent
> The footstep of a wild intent . . .

But I was not to be lone for long. From somewhere behind me came the cheerful sound of a horn and the grinding of gears. The next minute I was overtaken by another bus, this time a mini-bus (one of those useful words that remains the same in Welsh). It stopped and a chorus of friendly voices urged me aboard.

I squeezed myself into what I imagined to be a WI summer outing of some kind, or an Open University expedition. Perhaps Shelley was a more popular subject these days than I realized.

'No, no!' they told me. 'Today's the sale! No parking, so the auctioneers are running people up and down from the town.'

It seemed the house was only now going out of private hands and would soon become a school. Meanwhile the distinguished family who owned it for so long had turned over the entire contents for public auction.

'The whole of North Wales will be here!'

And so it was. At the top of the drive, the house was still invisible, this time because of the crowds and the marquee. The Welsh country sale to end all country sales was in full swing. The traditional scene was complete in every detail – the smell of crushed grass and hot canvas, the local constable at the entrance, perspiring in helmet and heavy moustache, steaming tea-urns on trestle tables, picnic baskets and family parties in the back rows. Glorious objects were being carried in and out by the porters, mahogany bureaux, ancestral paintings, and Georgian silver.

Leaving the serious bidding behind, I wandered among the flotsam and jetsam which would be sold at the end of the day. Here were the real relics of family life, tumbled out of every lumber-room and nursery cupboard to end up strewn like a shipwreck on the surrounding lawn – the frayed hammocks and the Edwardian croquet sets, old hip-baths, boxes of toy solders, a bust of Lloyd George and mysterious things like water-filters and honey extractors. A framed flag labelled 'Siege of Ladysmith' was propped up against a set of bagpipes and a keyed accordion. Whose was the 'Court Dress' in its leather case? And from what outposts of Empire had the native spears and harpoons been brought home to Wales, along with the stuffed baby crocodile, the elephant's foot umbrella-stand and other dusty trophies?

In the background, the empty house looked equally abandoned, the charming Italianate villa that had once been the toast of the parties from London summoned by the charismatic Madocks.

I found myself thinking of Hafod. Was this the way my own small paradise was to end, gutted of memories and handed over to strangers?

I brushed away the picture. I had after all come in search of the poet and that curious episode of attempted murder. With all attention on the sale, it might be the moment to slip through the elegant veranda and take a look inside.

The first reception room was stripped bare, down to its carved chimney-piece and peeling alcoves. Perhaps it was here that so many hopeful schemes had been hatched by the young couple, Harriet looking ahead to her first confinement, Bysshe rehearsing one of his revolutionary speeches, or reading aloud from his final draft of *Queen Mab*. Then, on a night of ferocious wind and rain, he found himself struggling with an armed intruder. The assailant fled, but later returned to make a second attack, so the story goes.

'I had been in bed three hours,' wrote Harriet to Hookham, 'when I heard a pistol go off. I immediately ran downstairs when I perceived that Bysshe's flannel gown had been shot through, and the window curtain. A man had thrust his arm thro' the glass and fired at him. Thank Heaven Mr Shelley happened to stand sideways. Had he stood fronting, the ball must have killed him.'

Shelley's letter to his publisher was more to the point. 'I have just escaped an atrocious assassination. Oh send me £20 if you have it! You will perhaps hear of me no more!'

I stood at a casement window which might well have been the scene of the crime. Had it been a neurotic hallucination, or even a ploy to escape from debt and disillusion? I put my hand on the frame.

'Yes, that's the window,' said a voice behind me.

The bluff elderly man seemed to know what was in my mind. A distant relative of the departing family, he told me there had once been a mark in the wainscot made by the bullet. But of course it was patched over long ago.

'There were those who said the shot was fired from inside by Shelley himself. But I'm not sure.' He shook his head. 'Wales was a wild place in those days, especially for a stranger with eccentric ideas.' He smiled to himself. 'Still is in parts.'

I wasn't sure either.

'There was always a streak of paranoia,' I said. Harriet knew about that, I thought. 'But, he certainly made enemies.'

My friend was looking out at the garden. 'I remember there used to be an old beech tree down there, an old giant of a tree. As children, we were always shown where the trunk had been slashed about with sword-marks. Shelley is said to have found a cavalry sabre in the house and went for the tree with it whenever his frustrations got too much for him. Then, about thirty years ago, it came crashing down in a storm. Caused quite a bit of damage to the roof. Perhaps Shelley was responsible for that too!'

Here the conversation ended. He was called away and I went out into the garden. Sadly there was no sign of a slashed-about tree trunk. But under another beech tree I came across a stone urn on a pedestal. A medallion of Ffestiniog slate was inscribed with the words, 'Percy Bysshe Shelley stayed here 1812–13 and completed *Queen Mab*. All things are recreated.'

I took the message away with me. At the time though the note of visionary optimism seemed far removed from reality. Without warning, at the age of fifty, my brother Renfrey was found dead of an embolism in the house he had lived in alone since my parents died. There had to be a clear-out of everything left behind in all those bulging cupboards and drawers. The task was at least a distraction from grief. Given the family passion for memorabilia, it turned into a minor archaeological excavation going down half a dozen layers from the 1940s to Victorian times, from ration-books and identity cards to souvenir programmes of the great queen's visit to Wrexham. The bundles of photographs and letters held me up for hours (my Ellis grandmother's dashed-off writing with the prophetic words, 'Baby June loves to talk but doesn't like walking.') Then, further back, there were the black-edged bereavement notes (a favourite nephew killed at Gallipoli) and the yellowing newspaper cuttings with endless lists of wedding presents, down to the last fish-knife.

Less fascinating were the hundred or so milk bottles stored 'for collection' in an outhouse by dear Renfrey, who was famous amongst his friends for his gifts of procrastination. His first car still stood in the garage, unused for years except by the wasps who always made their nest under the bonnet.

Once again there was much to be saved, including my father's books, my mother's china, my brother's records and one or two favourite pieces of furniture. Once again the Hafod sheds came into their own. Soon enough this latest consignment might have to be moved on with the rest of our things, if or when the time came for us to go.

Griff and Idwal voiced disbelief when the idea leaked out. They had been helping with the clearance, loading and unloading the yellow and black Cheetah. Last to come up was a small mahogany travelling-desk belonging to my great-grandfather, which was installed in my bedroom. Alas, it was firmly locked and there was no sign of a key.

'I'll find you one to fit,' Idwal offered. 'There's lots of old ones knocking around at home.'

'Or I could get it done in London,' I said, without thinking.

I caught an exchange of glances across the kitchen table.

'Is it true you're thinking of moving then?'

'Leaving Hafod?'

'Leaving Wales?'

There was mounting incredulity in their voices. I tried to explain that there was no definite plan as yet. It just seemed we had reached some kind of crossroads. So much was changing, the valley might well become a different place, might no longer feel like home to us. Such things happened. And now this new job at the BBC had come up. It would mean living full-time in London or nearby, buying a family-sized house there. So it made sense to find out the market value of Hafod to help us decide what to do.

'Couldn't you rent it out, use it for holidays?' said Griff.

It wasn't that kind of place, though, was it? All three of us agreed on that.

'Anyway,' I went on, rather feebly. 'People keep telling us we should be looking ahead. As you get older, living halfway up a mountain in Wales and at the top of sixty-five stairs in London isn't exactly sensible, they say.'

'Who are "they"?' muttered Idwal into his beard.

'Have you found somewhere else then?' Griff wanted to know.

'There's this place in Kent – ' I began.

'*Kent!*'

I might have been talking about California. There was not much point in going on to describe the comfortable house left to friends of ours by their parents. Before putting it up for sale, they kindly suggested we stay there for a week to see how we liked it. It was almost like being in the country, they said. There was a marvellous view of the Weald . . .

As I was to discover, the view of the Weald was the most unnerving part of the experience. Bereft of mountains, the Kentish horizons seemed as alien as a lunar landscape, so did the immaculate lawns, the mullioned windows and the sweeping gravelled driveway. Going in once or twice on the crowded commuter train to Victoria, I tried hard to adjust to the deafening silence of my fellow-prisoners. *Hiraeth* is the Welsh word for the way I was feeling – an overpowering homesickness that is almost physical.

Back at the flat, we both struggled vainly with the idea of becoming permanent exiles in the Home Counties. That night I had a disturbing dream. Not surprisingly, it began with a sale. I was back at Tan-yr-Allt, only this time the house was Hafod. On the auctioneer's rostrum was Benny the Bid and piled up around him on Idwal's steps were the familiar household contents, chattering crowds happily picking over the books and the pictures, the flowery china, even the photograph albums. 'Sold!' went the cry, as Benny's hammer went down on William Ellis's desk. At the back Miss Parry-Williams was triumphantly carrying away the missing half of Doctor Johnson's *Dictionary*. All this I could see from the gate. But I was not allowed to go through. A barrier had been erected, a border frontier with guards, and I had lost my passport . . .

The next morning R was amused by my account. It was hard to convey the threatening atmosphere of this nightmare, the sense of powerless frustration. It was still hanging over me when the telephone rang. My producer at Broadcasting House wanted me to come in to discuss details of the job proposal.

With hardly a pause, I heard myself say, 'I'm awfully sorry, but I'm afraid there's not much point.' Fumbling for explanations, I went on, 'I've decided I'm not really cut out to be a presenter on a current affairs programme, especially one going out live every day.'

I heard a long-suffering sigh. 'It's the idea of not being able to live in Wales, isn't it?'

He was an old friend who knew me only too well.

'Yes,' I said.

'Does that mean you're giving up radio altogether? Because there's another proposal that's just come up –

music and interviews with the great classical soloists, Ashkenazy and so on. To be called *Concerto*. Just a couple of series a year, recorded, of course.'

I took a deep breath. 'Yes, please,' I said.

'The fees should be useful anyway,' were his parting words. 'If you're going to keep up that crumbling old cottage of yours.'

It was a glorious moment to realize that, after all, nothing need change. Wales was still ours and our half-hearted efforts to be 'sensible' could be abandoned forthwith.

The very next day, as if by fate, something arrived to remind me how close to folly we had been. The over-keen estate agents sent me a specimen brochure for Hafod. I stared at the photo in disbelief. Taken in the depths of winter from an unfortunate angle in the lane, it showed a dingy white corner of the house (where the wall needed replastering), almost obscured by bare branches and dead weeds, with a close-up view of the sheds, a collapsing sheep-fence and the network of electric cables suspended from the telegraph pole.

Poor Hafod! It was rather like seeing a dearly-loved friend portrayed at a time of failing health in the obituary columns. But, as I comforted myself, it was all for the best. No prospective buyer would be tempted to make an early offer on this recommendation. Even so, there was no time to be lost. I sprang to the phone to cancel any suggestion that the property was coming up for sale.

The estate agents' number was engaged all morning. At lunchtime I got a train and was back in the valley by early evening. The taxi-driver seemed to baulk at the cattle-grid, so I got out to walk up the rest of the way. I was hailed by a shout from below. Young David emerged from the stables where he was milking.

'Want some?' he called as he scrambled up the bank with a can in his hand. His black hair was tousled, his overalls plastered with mud. There was a family likeness in that smile, a promise of continuity.

'Message from Megan,' he said. 'She's been with my mother at the village, back tomorrow. Please come round, she says.'

An elderly wall-eyed dog thrust himself forward from the rest of the gaggle at David's heels and politely put his nose into my hand.

'So Pero's not going to the town after all,' I said.

'Not yet anyway.' He laughed. 'And my *nain* wants to see you too. She and Auntie Gwyneth want to show you the new house.'

Turning up to Hafod, Pero kept me company with his usual game of dodging in and out of the fence. I took a deep breath of damp mountain air, caught the cry of the buzzard high up in the clouds, felt the old happiness begin to sink in. Until I got to the gate. A car was parked there. Then I remembered that, in all the excitement, I had completely forgotten that I had left a spare key at the estate agents' office. At the far end of the path a man and a woman were making their way into the house.

To come face to face with would-be buyers was more than I had bargained for at this particular moment. On an impulse I made a quick detour up the steps to the back of the house, praying they would not follow up their inspection of the house with a tour of the garden.

But after ten minutes inside, it seemed they had seen quite enough. Piercing English voices rose up clearly in the evening stillness as they made their way down the path again.

'A power cut! Honestly! Does it often happen up here, do you think?'

'Shouldn't wonder, out in the sticks like this. Wouldn't do my computers any good.'

'Strange people they must be. All that second-hand junk. And the awful wallpaper.'

'Poky rooms too. Might be better without all those books, though.'

'Did you notice the water was a funny brown colour?'

'And that dead mouse in the bath! Hardly the place for our jacuzzi.'

By now they were at the gate. I kept my head down behind the blackberry bushes.

'Terrible jungle up there, isn't it?' I heard the lady remark in crushing tones. 'Still, we could have concrete put down in the front, I suppose.'

'And if we could get a real knock-down price for it . . . ' Then, as the gate clanged to behind them – 'Damn! I've trodden in something!'

'It's the sheep. We'd have to get rid of those for a start. Why can't Welsh farmers keep them in fields like everyone else?'

The voices faded with the sound of the car driving away. I couldn't get into the house fast enough. Gwen had laid a fire. Within minutes it was ablaze and the catalogue consigned to the flames. Then there were phone calls to be made, first to the agents, the next one to R.

'The hawthorn's out,' I told him when we'd finished laughing. 'And Griff's filled in the holes in the track.'

'I'll be up the day after tomorrow.'

On the table, inside the souvenir mug from Pwllheli, was a small key. Idwal had tied a label to it that read simply, 'Try this'. So I did. The moment of opening the desk took me back to that day when I managed to let myself into Hafod, taking possession through the back door all those years ago. Now, as then, there was treasure inside. The neat rows of black leather diaries went back to 1869. As I started to read William Ellis's microscopic handwriting, I knew I had discovered a private passion that would take me well into the next few years. With my great-grandfather's blessing I might even begin to write my own story of those vanished lives . . .

If I could have seen still further ahead, I would have found that our own lives were once again to be taken over by Hafod. More than anything it was to be a haven in times of trouble, when change came in a way I had never imagined. Developing heart problems, R was to take early retirement and recover his health here under Dr Ivor's ministrations. Some years later, I was diagnosed with breast cancer. After surgery and long weeks of treatment, Hafod once again provided its own healing spell.

By this time Vanessa was married. There was snow on the mountain when she and Hugo brought their newborn offspring, Polly, home from the hospital to Hafod where she spent the first year of her life. Then they moved to a farmhouse near Corwen in the next valley and Polly came to visit us most days. Like her Welsh grandmother she enjoyed talking. 'Sheep' was an early word, so was 'owl' and 'steps', in one mangled form or another. Not long afterwards, as she stumped up the path from the gate, I heard her announce to herself, 'This *my* house!'

And so, in Shelley's words, 'All things are recreated'.

INDEX